Bedbug

Animal
Series editor: Jonathan Burt

Already published

Albatross Graham Barwell · *Ant* Charlotte Sleigh · *Ape* John Sorenson · *Badger* Daniel Heath Justice
Bat Tessa Laird · *Bear* Robert E. Bieder · *Beaver* Rachel Poliquin · *Bedbug* Klaus Reinhardt
Bee Claire Preston · *Beetle* Adam Dodd · *Bison* Desmond Morris · *Camel* Robert Irwin
Cat Katharine M. Rogers · *Chicken* Annie Potts · *Cockroach* Marion Copeland · *Cow* Hannah Velten
Crocodile Dan Wylie · *Crow* Boria Sax · *Deer* John Fletcher · *Dog* Susan McHugh · *Dolphin* Alan Rauch
Donkey Jill Bough · *Duck* Victoria de Rijke · *Eagle* Janine Rogers · *Eel* Richard Schweid
Elephant Dan Wylie · *Falcon* Helen Macdonald · *Flamingo* Caitlin R. Kight · *Fly* Steven Connor
Fox Martin Wallen · *Frog* Charlotte Sleigh · *Giraffe* Edgar Williams · *Goat* Joy Hinson
Gorilla Ted Gott and Kathryn Weir · *Guinea Pig* Dorothy Yamamoto · *Hare* Simon Carnell
Hedgehog Hugh Warwick · *Hippopotamus* Edgar Williams · *Horse* Elaine Walker · *Hyena* Mikita Brottman
Kangaroo John Simons · *Leech* Robert G. W. Kirk and Neil Pemberton · *Leopard* Desmond Morris
Lion Deirdre Jackson · *Lizard* Boria Sax · *Llama* Helen Cowie · *Lobster* Richard J. Kin
Monkey Desmond Morris · *Moose* Kevin Jackson · *Mosquito* Richard Jones · *Moth* Matthew Gandy
Mouse Georgie Carroll · *Octopus* Richard Schweid · *Ostrich* Edgar Williams · *Otter* Daniel Allen
Owl Desmond Morris · *Oyster* Rebecca Stott · *Parrot* Paul Carter · *Peacock* Christine E. Jackson
Penguin Stephen Martin · *Pig* Brett Mizelle · *Pigeon* Barbara Allen · *Rabbit* Victoria Dickenson
Rat Jonathan Burt · *Rhinoceros* Kelly Enright · *Salmon* Peter Coates · *Sardine* Trevor Day
Scorpion Louise M. Pryke · *Seal* Victoria Dickenson · *Shark* Dean Crawford · *Sheep* Philip Armstrong
Skunk Alyce Miller · *Snail* Peter Williams · *Snake* Drake Stutesman · *Sparrow* Kim Todd
Spider Katarzyna and Sergiusz Michalski · *Swallow* Angela Turner · *Swan* Peter Young
Tiger Susie Green · *Tortoise* Peter Young · *Trout* James Owen · *Vulture* Thom van Dooren
Walrus John Miller and Louise Miller · *Whale* Joe Roman · *Wild Boar* Dorothy Yamamoto
Wolf Garry Marvin · *Woodpecker* Gerard Gorman · *Zebra* Christopher Plumb and Samuel Shaw

Bedbug

Klaus Reinhardt

REAKTION BOOKS

Published by
REAKTION BOOKS LTD
Unit 32, Waterside
44–48 Wharf Road
London N1 7UX, UK
www.reaktionbooks.co.uk

First published 2018
Copyright © Klaus Reinhardt 2018

Printed and bound in China by 1010 Printing International Ltd

A catalogue record for this book is available from the British Library

ISBN 978 1 78023 973 6

Contents

Foreword

Few animals, few objects even, evoke such profound feelings of horror, fear and fright as bedbugs. Mention 'bedbug' and be sure to send shivers down people's spines. There were times when it was impolite to even say the b-word in public for fear it would elicit the bugs to enter one's home or facilitate their thriving. The sight of a single bedbug in their surroundings has kept people mentally occupied for weeks – and it still does, whether ordinary people, world-renowned poets, political leaders or other celebrities. Today, reports of hotel rooms with bedbugs or pictures and videos of heavily infested apartments go around the world in seconds. Bedbugs are serious business. You can joke about cockroaches in an apartment, or fleas, but you don't make a joke about bedbugs in someone's house. No, you simply don't. Well, until very recently, that is. Now bedbugs are becoming more of a normal thing – allegedly one in five people in the u.s. has had experiences with them – and the first cartoons portraying bedbugs in a funny, even likeable, way are appearing. Or, as we shall see, they are reappearing. We have lived through such times before – actually, worse ones – and we will see how humans coped then.

Uninvited, bedbugs invade your private space – your bed. Without asking, they help themselves to your very own bodily fluid, your blood, and in order to make the valuable liquid flow

A female bedbug as illustrated in the Natural History Museum's *Economic Series*.

more easily they spit into it. Into your blood! They leave you exposed in the most vulnerable way, naked in your bed. The bites cause itches and rashes that drive you crazy, robbing you of what you most need, your sleep. These characteristics make the bedbug a perfect representation of an alien, something evil, the Other par excellence, a depiction that can be kept alive for various reasons and by several means. One way of fuelling the fear is to personalize it by addressing the reader directly – *your* bed, *your* blood – as I have just done in the previous sentences. In this way I imposed personal imaginative responses to an infestation, rather than using less scaremongering terms such as *one's* bed. We will look into other tactics by which the fear is kept simmering.

The second part of this book will examine a recently emerged issue, the sex life of the bedbug, which is no less disturbing than its other habits, such as binge-drinking of blood, starving for a year, or being the surrogate of everything unwanted. The process of 'traumatic insemination' has been used by scientists to study evolution. The popularization of their findings by the press – after all, sex sells – has led to dozens, perhaps hundreds of cartoons, plays, radio programmes and blog entries on the topic of traumatic insemination. As is often the case with the nether regions of the body, comments on the sex life of the bedbug are made with an attempt at humour. They may be funny, but do these comments and cartoons perhaps reveal something in addition? Portraying bedbugs as lustful little copulation machines is an interesting continuation of a thread starting with the explicit descriptions of the bedbug's sexual activities depicted in tales of the North American Hopi and extending to current-day novels or Internet comics.

The third part explores how the personal fear of bedbugs was institutionalized and how it elicited societal responses, such as the development of pest control and bedbug research. Our sense of estrangement towards bedbugs and their secretive lifestyles seem

Detail from an educational wall poster by Albrecht Hase showing a male bedbug, c. 1930.

Fig. 7 Männchen
(30 fach vergrößert)

to have become manifest in a recurrent tendency to liken our enemies to bedbugs. Throughout history, groups of people, often foreign, have been described as blood-sucking vermin, lice and bugs that need to be kept at bay or, in extreme cases, eradicated. The resulting creation of the alien Other has been associated with genocide and mass murder on an unbelievable scale, culminating in the incomprehensibly anti-humane perfection of anti-Semitism in the Holocaust. Experiments on bedbugs led to the development of the most extensively produced man-made exterminating substance in human history, and a most potent insecticide: Zyklon B. A cruel irony that only real history can provide is that this substance was developed in the laboratories of Fritz Haber: German patriot, 'father' of the German gas war, winner of the Nobel Prize and Jew.

As bedbugs frighten most people by the mere mention of their name, those that actually work with bedbugs must, almost by definition, be considered brave and fearless, a myth that these carriers of public admiration do not hurry to quell. Public attention fuels further public attention, resulting in competition, disputes and even plagiarism to crawl out of their dark corners – in bedbug science, in bedbug fiction and in bedbug pictures. Yet the bedbug has left many other traces in human culture, language and knowledge. This book investigates how, through the centuries, people felt about them, how they coped with them, and what they did to counter what is undoubtedly an animal worth examining in more detail.

1 Bug Diversity

So what is this animal that makes very few people – me, for example – happy, but causes most to shudder? What is this animal that few people in the Western world recognize, but causes more mental despair than any other human parasite?[1] Despite this alleged accolade, the bedbug is not even dangerous. I will introduce an animal that lent its name to pretty much every other bug, including the stomach bug, the computer bug and the electronic bug.

The word 'bug' supposedly derives from the Welsh *bwag*, meaning goblin, linking it to Shakespeare's early use in, for example, 'With ho! Such bugs and goblins in my life' (*Hamlet*, v.ii). However, much more frequently Shakespeare referred to fleas or lice. *Bug* may also come from the Arabic *al-bukk*, a term seafarers might have brought to the English language.

Some associations live on in our daily life in the form of the eighteenth-century 'snug as a bug in a rug', 'cute as a bug's ear' or the 'shutterbug'. By contrast, the seemingly innocent 'bug-a-boo' made by parents to their small children already contains some element of fright. It is doubtful that this term exclusively serves as an innocent joke. It may be a transition to 'bugbear'. 'Bug' often means a quirk or refers to something that doesn't work, culminating in the overtly offensive 'bughouse', 'bug-eyed' or even to 'bugger off'. The exclamation 'humbug' can be used ambivalently, in either a friendly or derogative way.

A study in Germany and Britain asked whether people would recognize this animal. In both countries, about one in eight participants correctly stated it is a bedbug.

Bugs are not fleas, lice or ticks, neither mites nor flies. Certainly these all suck blood (at least their females do), and all but ticks are insects. Yet biologically they are more unrelated than fish and dolphins.

What are bugs, then? There are many types of bug and many ways to characterize them. In the United States and Australia pretty much everything crawling, creepy or small is called a bug, including cockroaches, bees and mosquitoes, but also disease-related bacteria and viruses. This is not so much the case in Great Britain, where the term is used more restrictively, although 'stomach bug' also exists. I wonder if this less restricted use of the word 'bug' might be related to the possibility that among the people that left Britain for Australia or the United States, many had lived under conditions where bedbugs were the most commonly encountered small creature. Or were the bedbug experiences on emigrant ships of such intensity that they left a lasting trace in the language?

Bugs can also be used in reference to the 40,000 species of true bugs, more formally called Heteroptera. The Greek words *hetero* ('different') and *pteros* ('wing') capture the fact that the bugs' forewings and hindwings are of different shapes. These heteropteran fellows can be beautiful and nothing like the ugly

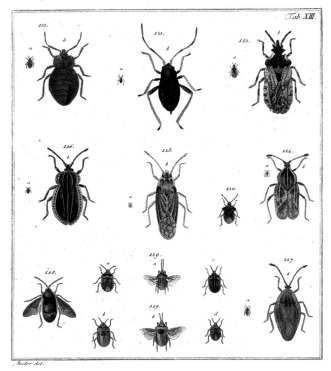

Émile Blanchard, illustration from *Histoire naturelle des insectes orthoptères, névroptères, hémiptères, hyménoptères, lépidoptères et diptères*, vol. III (1851), showing the bedbug *Cimex lectularius* and other true bugs.

Johann Friedrich Wolff and Johann Philip Wolff, illustration from *Icones cimicum descriptionibus illustratae*, book 1, vol. i, tab xiii, showing a selection of true bugs, 1800.

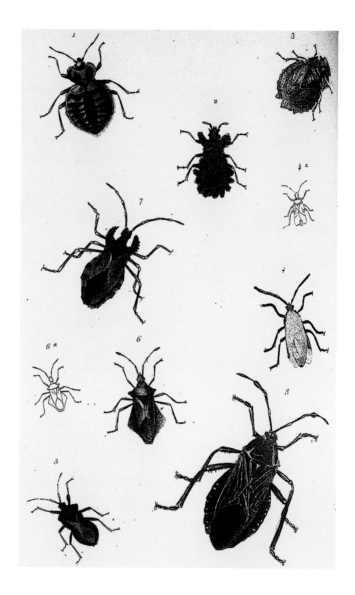

or evil connotation that 'bug' usually represents. They may be sapsuckers or they may ambush other insects and then suck their victim's juices. They live by the water and skate on ponds, crawl over the mud, walk underwater on the beds of rivers and creeks, or hang upside down below the water's surface. Some of these latter types even make noises, an unusual feature of bugs. Relative to their body size, indeed, these bugs are the loudest of all animals, louder than elephants. Other Heteroptera live in, on, or around plants, including on the roots and under the bark of trees, and use their beak (or proboscis, or rostrum, as it is also called) to pierce flower buds, stems, leaves, fruits and pretty much any other parts of a plant to extract their favourite liquid. Some of these true bugs defend themselves by releasing a nasty substance when pestered ('stink bugs'), and so smell unpleasant when they are being squashed. They can also leave a smell where they have laid their eggs. If, for example, the esteemed reader may kindly

Cimex druraei illustrated in G.W.F. Panzer's Translation into German of Drury's Exotic Insects (1785).

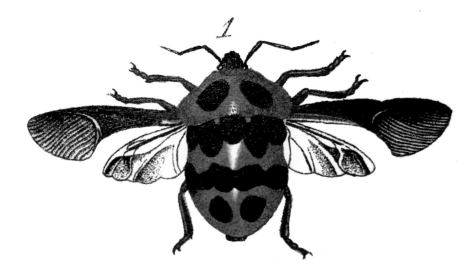

John Curtis, 19th-century illustration from *British Entomology*. The common bedbug is depicted along with a plant, the garlic mustard, and line drawings of fine anatomical details of the bedbug.

A beautiful plant-sucking bug, *Lygaeus equestris*. The species was chosen as Insect of the Year in Austria and Germany, 2007.

admit to having occasionally experienced a strange chemical taste when eating wild raspberries, he or she is likely to have crunched a bug, or a bug egg, if that is a more comfortable thought. At the other extreme, I found that the large North American species *Leptoglossus occidentalis*, which feeds on pine cones and is currently invading Europe, emitted a lovely strawberry-like, fruity smell when I caught it. Other heteropterans live on plants that humans rely upon, such as cereals, fruit, rice, ornamental plants or vegetables. Being a home for bugs can be problematic for the plants, as well as for the humans who eat or use them. Particular issues arise from those bug species that have the habit of allowing deadly plant viruses to inhabit the tip of their beaks, and so transport them into every plant the bugs pierce. Generally though, the vast majority of bug species mind their own business more or less quietly. Some of these are regularly eaten by humans, such as the giant water bug. Others, often unappreciated, feed on insects that damage crops, or spend their lives caring for their young. In 2007 one bug species must have felt particularly honoured when it was chosen as 'Insect of the Year' in Germany, Switzerland and Austria.

Some of these quiet and little talked about bugs possess a secluded beauty, a beauty that has served to alert people to the threats of nuclear leaks. A year after the Chernobyl nuclear plant disaster, for example, bugs observed in northern Europe showed dramatically distorted bodies resulting from mutations associated with nuclear radiation.

Finally, bugs are also the *real* bugs, the bedbugs. Their name has been applied to all the other 40,000 species, because few bugs were considered to have sufficient significance to warrant their own name. Our intimate companion was granted the explanatory specification of its habitat type – the bed – in its name only after other bugs had received sufficient attention to justify their own name, such as the water bug, flower bug or fire bug.

So, what are *real* bedbugs, then? Some say they are all of the one hundred or so species of the family Cimicidae that scientists have currently identified. In this book, we will meet only a few other species, their living rooms and their heroic discoverers. Most species of the Cimicidae are extremely rare creatures, known from only one or a few individuals identified from a single location in the world and never seen again since their discovery in the 1960s. This rarity is not likely to improve much as the Cimicidae are reclusive by nature. Not only that, they live in places that hardly qualify as anyone's favourite holiday destination, such as bat caves lined with knee-deep guano, or boiling hot, moist caves with large colonies of birds or fruit-eating bats (the fruit-eating part here illustrates the type of smell to be expected from what the bats deposit in these caves). Later, in Chapter Six, we will turn to other forms of heroic encounters with bedbugs. Some bedbugs live in swallow nests, others in the edible nests of swiftlets in Southeast Asian jungle caves. My own favourite is the ultra-specialized *Latrocimex*. They are found only in South America, where the trees in particular mangrove stands are large enough to contain the holes needed to harbour the fish-eating bats whose blood *Latrocimex* likes. Some bedbug species are small, others are large, most are brownish and all suck blood. To catch those species, special arrangements sometimes have to be made.

The *real* bedbugs, however, the ones mostly found in and near our beds, belong to just two species, more or less. One resides in the tropics and is called *Cimex hemipterus*, while the other, *Cimex lectularius*, dwells in temperate zones. The latter species is the one that is currently spreading. As much of world literature is primarily based in temperate zones, this species happens to be the more prominent in fiction.[?] The tropical bedbug is currently conquering

The size range of the bedbug family, showing a nymph of the very rare and large *Primicimex cavernis* alongside the common bedbug (in the centre) and the cactus-dwelling *Hesperocimex*.

19

northern Australia and the southern United States, but for the most part it remains a fellow of the tropics, being hardly found in Europe or most of North America. We can, therefore, put to rest the myth that we, the clean Europeans and North Americans, bring them back from our holidays in the unclean tropics. There is a third type of bed-dwelling bug, *Leptocimex boueti*, but apart from the possibility of a surprise visit, this species has hardly been heard of since 1913. It lives, or lived, in West Africa, where in the 1960s it was claimed to prefer biting the African natives rather than European visitors.[3]

Bedbugs, that is the two *Cimex* types described above, while considered disgusting and appalling by the majority of the world's population, are by many standards also among the world's most unusual animals. Some of their behaviours and other expressions of living are outright bizarre, at least by human criteria.

The tropical (left) and the temperate bedbug (right) look very much alike. Here, two males are depicted.

Bed Bug

Mistaken identity. Unlike what is stated on this children's card game, the species depicted is not the common bedbug. The species probably belongs to the genus *Leptocimex*, which is known from very few places in the world. The game was published in 1976. The publisher does not seem to exist anymore and the photographer could not be located. The exact location where this animal lived and what species it belongs to would have been an interesting contribution by a card game to science.

For a start, bedbugs lost their wings during evolution and cannot fly, so they need to attach to something, or someone, in order to cover large distances. Bedbugs also don't eat. They only drink. They drink blood, and nothing but blood. This is now firmly established, even though the grand old master of bedbug biology, John Southall, claimed to have seen bedbugs sucking the juice from plants and wood. All members of the bedbug family drink blood: mum, dad and the kids. Bedbugs have five nymphal stages and a new stage can only be reached after a blood meal has been acquired in between. Only the eggs are more frugal: they are happy with a bit of air to breathe.

21

The preferred type of blood for bedbugs in most parts of the world is mainly that of humans. In central Europe and Asia Minor, however, bedbugs are still found naturally in caves, as well as in churches or other more modern caves, as long as there are bats in residence, too. In these cases *Cimex lectularius* prefers the blood of bats, a taste preference it shares with other species of bedbug. This shared taste preference is why most biologists currently assume that the human-blood drinkers evolved from bat-blood drinkers. We don't know why or how this happened, but an educated guess is that the specialization of the bat-liking bugs on to humans is linked to the times when these bedbugs started to live in caves and regularly feast on humans. Bedbugs that live on the blood of humans also differ in some of their genes from those that live on bat blood.[4] Such genetic differences have arisen because drinkers of bat blood and human blood have 'not

Just hatched! Nymphs of the bedbug after their first blood meal. The skin is still translucent and the blood clearly visible. This blood meal will now provide enough food for the bedbug nymphs to achieve the first moult.

met' for a long time – in other words, they have not interbred with each other. In turn, to not have interbred means either they did not meet and mate, or they did mate but this did not result in young. Currently it is estimated that the bat-drinkers and the human-drinkers separated a quarter of a million years ago.[5] This is interesting, as it is long before modern humans (*Homo sapiens*) left Africa. Would then, therefore, *Cimex lectularius* have sucked on pre-modern humans, such as *Homo erectus* or the Neanderthals? If bat-drinkers and human-drinkers had separated in Africa, one would probably more likely expect *Cimex lectularius* in wild bat roosts in Africa, and not in Europe as we observe now. We can probably expect more exciting news on this point.

Another interesting and unresolved question is how blood-sucking bugs evolved from ancestors that either sucked out the juices of other insects (assassin bugs, for example) or that sucked

Shed skins are left behind by moulting bedbugs, for example on the carpet.

plant sap. The current idea that the first Cimicidae obtained their lifeblood from bats gets quite shaky, because the first Cimicidae were captured in amber about 100 million years ago, that is more than 30 million years before the first flaps of the first proto-bats on Earth.

Despite having a preference for a type of blood, bedbugs are not very strict in their diet when opportunities are limited. They will drink pretty much any creature's blood or, more precisely, any warm-blooded creature's blood. In zoos or households, for example, bedbugs do not refuse a good drink from animals they do not usually encounter, such as pika hares, storks, dogs, cats or rabbits. If cold-blooded geckos are kept warm enough in their terrarium, bedbugs do not abstain from helping themselves. Chickens and other birds are also high on the list. For example, a pigeon bug is known, a bedbug species that is very closely related to our bedbug and lives mainly on pigeon blood, though it may be close to extinction as hardly any have been recorded over the last fifty years or so. The pigeon bug can produce offspring with the normal bedbug, which biologists usually take as a sign to place them within the same species. The fact that the two types can inter-breed has led to an alternative hypothesis that the human-blood drinkers may also have evolved from pigeon-blood drinkers.[6] Indeed, the relationship between humans and pigeons has been close and has lasted for millennia. Several religions regard pigeons as holy animals and their lofts are guarded by designated people whose blood would provide an ideal, though currently theoretical, vessel for bedbugs to hop onto other humans. This host shift, as the hopping process is called formally, may have been augmented by an availability of chicken blood. Chickens have a similarly long and intimate relationship with man, and represent a sub-stantial food reservoir to bugs as well. Hen houses covered with bedbugs 'as completely as with wallpaper', as Johann Heinrich

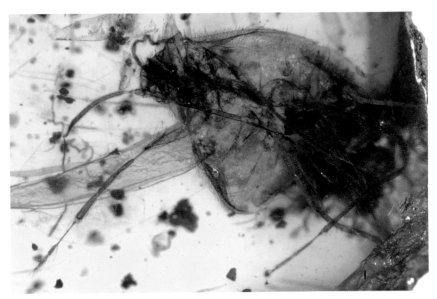

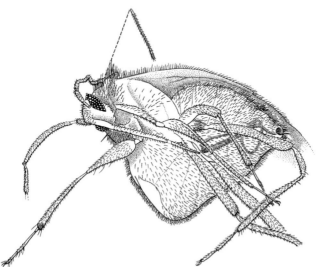

Quasicimex, a 100-million-year-old fossil from the mid-Cretaceous period, the supposed mother of all bedbug species, or father in this case. The interpretation of the structures is shown below.

A North American
bedbug species
feeding on blood
from a bat's nose.

Jördens observed in 1801, are testimony to a close relationship
between bugs, chickens and humans that continues to the current
day in the form of sophisticated, though largely secret, control
programmes to clear chicken farms of bedbugs.[7]

2 Bug Years

Let us now turn to what we know more directly about bedbug history rather than from calculating how much the genes of various bedbugs differ from one another. Bedbugs lived in ancient Egypt at least 3,600 years ago – a single specimen was extracted from the so-called workmen's village built to supply labour to Akhenaten's new capital at Tell el-Amana.[1] In England bedbugs showed their presence in the remains of a second- or third-century Romano-British settlement at Alcester, Warwickshire; in excavations of the Saxon levels at Fishergate, Norwich; and in Cutlers Gardens, Spitalfields, in eighteenth-century London. At the Cutlers Gardens site, a single bedbug was found in exactly one out of sixteen samples of soil weighing 1 kilogram each. The soil layer corresponded to deposits of the year 1750, a time when many written records depict London as teeming with bedbugs. This puts into perspective the finding of the single fossilized bedbug in ancient Egypt; perhaps the discovery of this single bug highlights that substantial bedbug infestations occurred in old Egypt as much as the recorded spells against them do.

Continuing with the historical timeline, bedbugs were also mentioned by Pliny the Elder, while Aristophanes' plays contain the oldest reports of bedbugs in fiction. In *The Frogs* the travelling god of wine and joy, Dionysus, seeks the hostel with the fewest bedbugs, which was normal in ancient Greece. Later, the bedbug appears in an evocation by the apostle John to the bedbugs to stay outside for the night (Leucius' Acts of John in the New Testament, around AD 200) and in the Talmud.

Recently two bedbugs were found in the lead coffin of Queen Edith or Eadgyth (910–946), which was moved to Magdeburg Cathedral in the sixteenth century.[2] She had been brought up in the Saxon kingdoms of Wessex and Mercia and travelled to Germany in 929 to marry the future German emperor Otto I (912–973). Perhaps the bedbugs were buried with Edith in 946, drawn by the warmth of her body and clothes. This would make it the earliest bedbug recorded in central Europe, older than an often-repeated but difficult-to-trace record from eleventh-century Strasbourg. My personal suggestion, however, is that the bug crawled into the lead coffin later, seeking the darkness: a crack in the lead would have been quite wide enough for a bug to enter.

A semi-fossilized bedbug excavated in a workmen's village in ancient Egypt, from about 1500 BC.

An illustration from a 1536 edition of the medical text *Hortus sanitatis*. The picture says it shows lice, but aspects of the body shape and the antennae resemble bedbugs, making it possibly the first depiction in history.

The original association between Edith and bedbugs would then be a little more doubtful, which might perhaps explain the startlingly low coverage in the English-speaking press of the discovery that a German queen of English origin had supposedly lived with bedbugs, and was buried with some of them.

If we leave the area of speculation and return to history, the bedbug is mentioned as a pest almost globally in natural history writings between the thirteenth and seventeenth centuries.[3] In the Chinese *Cheng Huai Lu*, wild rhubarb is claimed to be effective against bedbugs as early as 1204.[4] In Germany, the *Wandlaus* (wall-louse) became known by its current name *Wanze* in about 1450,[5] while in England the wall-louse became known as 'bug' around the same time or a little after. The Coverdale Bible (1535) translates Psalms 91:5 as 'Thou shalt not nede to be afrayed for eny

Title page of John
Southall's *A Treatise
of Buggs* (1730).

A
TREATISE
OF
BUGGS:

SHEWING

When and How they were firſt brought
into *England*. How they are brought
into and infect Houſes.

Their Nature, ſeveral Foods, Times and
Manner of Spawning and Propagating in this
Climate.

Their great INCREASE accounted for, by
Proof of the Numbers each Pair produce in a
Seaſon.

REASONS given why all Attempts hitherto
made for their Deſtruction have proved
ineffectual.

VULGAR ERRORS concerning them refuted.

That from *September* to *March* is the beſt Seaſon for
their total Deſtruction, demonſtrated by Reaſon, and
proved by Facts.

Concluding with

DIRECTIONS for ſuch as have them not already, how
to avoid them; and for thoſe that have them, how to
deſtroy them.

By *JOHN SOUTHALL*,

Maker of the Nonpareil Liquor for deſtroying *Buggs* and
Nits, living at the *Green Poſts* in the *Green Walk* near
Faulcon-ſtairs, *Southwark*.

LONDON: Printed for J. ROBERTS, near the *Oxford-Arms*
in *Warwick-Lane*. M.DCC.XXX.

(Price One Shilling.)

bugges by night'.[6] There are also mentions in Edmund Spenser's *Faerie Queene* (1590), and we have already noted Shakespeare's reference to bugs. In 1583 the pioneering biologist Thomas Penny was able to reassure two women in Mortlake that the marks they thought were signs of plague were only bedbug bites. From the same time, the Chinese herbal book *Bencao gangmu*, published in 1590, reports that bedbugs can be found in almost every house north and south of the Yangtze river.

Just before 1600, in Bury St Edmunds, Suffolk, where some 380 years later disputes about bedbugs were resolved by unusual means in Clive Sinclair's wonderful short story 'Bedbugs', the composer John Wilbye set the words of an anonymous poet, 'these are but bugs to breed amazing', in his madrigal 'Thus saith my Cloris bright'. Thomas Muffet's *Theatrum insectorum* (1634), published thirty years after his death, mentions wall lice briefly. John Southall's hallmark *A Treatise of Buggs* appeared in 1730. Andrew Cooke of Holborn Hill advertised his services in 1775 as 'Bugg-destroyer of Her Majesty': back then, apparently, Queen Charlotte was not overly ashamed of having bedbugs. I imagine the situation in Buckingham Palace might be slightly different today. Across London, Cooke claimed to have cleared bugs from 16,000 beds. What is surprising, and I have not found an answer to the puzzle, is that after about 1700 Southall appears to be the only natural history scholar to mention the bedbug, even in passing. Has natural history moved on to the extravagant, ignoring the ordinary and leaving references to bedbugs to others?

It was not only London that was heaving with bedbugs, as reformist writers like Henry Mayhew (1812–1887) testified. Bedbugs are mentioned from Liverpool to the Isle of Wight, taking in Sheffield, Coventry and Manchester, showing that Southall's assertion that 'in Inland-Towns, Buggs are hardly known' was no longer true. Especially rich sources of knowledge, extensively

Jane Carlyle (1801–1866). Through her extensive diary-keeping activities, we are unusually well informed about the extent of bedbugs in London and other parts of England in the 19th century.

discussed in a superb article by L.O.J. Boynton, are the letters and diaries of Jane Carlyle, the wife of the celebrated writer Thomas Carlyle.[7] After they moved to London from Scotland in 1834 she mentioned that 'few houses here are without' bugs. Mayhew describes a visit to the 'Bug-trap' in Water-lane, Sheffield, 'which from time immemorial has been the name of the most renowned lodging-house in perhaps any locality'.[8] It is probably coincidence that about a hundred years after this observation Sheffield became an important centre for bedbug research, and again after a further sixty years.

In the Americas, John Southall reported being bitten in Jamaica in 1726, and Pehr Kalm met many bedbugs in the French and English colonies in 1748. The Hopi, native to North America, had probably known bedbugs for longer because they have their own word for them, totally unrelated to Spanish, English or French. Further examination, however, suggests that *pesets'ola* possibly refers to another species, the Mexican chicken bug (*Haematosiphon inodorus*), rather than the bedbug as we know it.[9] The Mexican chicken bug, before entering chicken coops and earning its name, was a parasite on the chicks of eagles and other raptors. As their stories assert, *pesets'ola* and the Hopi met frequently. This is not surprising given the close relationship of the Hopi with eagles, where eagle chicks become part of the enlarged clan family.

It was in Europe between 1850 and the mid-1940s that the bedbug came to the forefront. The situation of guesthouses in France teeming with bedbugs is richly illustrated in *La Grande*

A petroglyph engraved on rocks of the Second Mesa in Hopi land, Arizona. The petroglyph shows a Hopi eagle dancer about to be bitten.

Symphonie héroïque des punaises (The Great Heroic Symphony of Bedbugs, 1877), an almost Dadaistic play by Nadar (Gaspard-Félix Tournachon) and Charles Bataille.[10] In Britain there was an outcry in the 1930s after the Ministry of Health published information about the extent of infestations,[11] at the same time as hundreds of pest controllers worked throughout the city of Berlin.[12] It was estimated that one-third of apartments in Berlin, Oslo, Stockholm and London were infested: in some parts of London and Berlin the infestation spread to all houses. Oslo employed inspectors to certify that apartments were bug-free when tenants moved out.

There was also a good deal of travel among the bedbugs in Europe. Courtroom reporter and author Theodor Fontane travelled from Hamburg to London on the infested steamship *Countess of Lonsdale*, but could not find release in his 'infested sleeping cave called a bedroom' in a hotel in Finsbury Square.[13] The ship that ferried the famous German naturalist Ernst Haeckel from Tenerife to Lanzarote was infested, as were his accommodations on both islands.[14]

Fifteen years after his novel *The Count of Monte Cristo* appeared, Alexandre Dumas went in search of real adventure. His travels to the Caucasus in 1859 provide some interesting records of bedbugs, which he encountered in many places while pondering the pleasure they would have in biting the thin and tender skin of a European rather than the 'rough bark' of a Cossack.[15] Further north and east, there are few historical travel, scientific or hunting reports about Siberia that do not mention bedbugs. Anton Chekhov, for example, met them everywhere on his way to Sakhalin in 1890, where he investigated the conditions in tsarist prisons and observed that it was impossible for prisoners to obey the order to keep themselves free of bugs.[16] George Kennan also travelled through Siberia, in his case to study *katorga*, the tsarist system of forced labour. He complained about gigantic numbers of bedbugs keeping him awake, and how 'every night I killed fifteen or twenty bugs on my desk' – a figure that is only 'gigantic' if he was a rather unsuccessful bug hunter.[17]

Ships of the U.S. Navy needed regular disinfection.[18] U.S. courts were kept busy ruling on what to do in cases of infestation: in 1887 it was decided that a rent reduction was not justified because bedbugs should not be a surprise to anyone renting an apartment in New York. Fifty years later, however, landlords were deemed responsible for keeping their apartments free of vermin.[19]

Some reports even pass the realm of imagination. In Hitler's concentration camps the bedbugs robbed the imprisoned slaves of their sleep, their last chance of privacy and, in a vicious circle, their last opportunity to generate strength to resist their oppressors. Called the 'eleventh plague of Terezín', the bedbugs forced women to sleep in the open on the ground.[20] Recently discovered graffiti-like drawings and poems on the walls of houses in Terezín/ Theresienstadt show the diversity of nationalities present at that time. One reads:

I cannot sleep
Chapman gets up at three
Honyny sleeps till five
And Picka till half six.
Just the bedbugs are on duty
For the entire night

The prisoners' ability to keep a sense of humour while penned up in appalling living conditions in Terezín, both for an undetermined period of time and facing an unknown destination, is a testament to human fortitude.

Detailed research into bedbugs was now under way, too. Kenneth Mellanby carried out precisely designed experiments at

A cartoon from
c. 1890 showing
the severe situation
in New York.

BRER THULDY'S STATUE
LIBERTY FRIGHTENIN DE WORLD.
To be stuck up on Bedbugs Island - Jarsey Flats, opposit de United States.

(Only Authorized Edition.)

the Sorby Research Institute in Sheffield to find out how bedbugs reproduced, how they kept their water balance, and at what time of day bedbugs were most active. C. G. Johnson worked intensely at the London School of Hygiene and Tropical Medicine on how temperature affected reproduction and the ecology of the bedbug. He even built a small experimental hut to help keep track of how bedbugs distribute themselves in houses. In Berlin, Albrecht Hase, Heinrich Kemper, Ernst Janisch and Erich Titschack pursued intensive research into egg laying, ageing and blood sucking, some appeasing the terminology of the time as the 'biology of races' or 'age degeneration' (*Altersentartung*), paralleling the derogatory terms also applied to art and music.

Infestation rates in England and Germany decreased from the 1930s to the 1950s: by soon after 1950 little was happening in the world of the bedbug. It is not clear why bedbugs started to decline, although in England this may be the result of changes in housing conditions, particularly following the Housing Act of 1930, which gave British local authorities greater powers, promoting slum clearances and the start of huge rebuilding efforts. Throughout the 1980s there was little sign of any increase in infestations and this situation continued into the mid-1990s. That is in the West, of course. In Africa nobody talked of a bedbug increase or decline, but their abundance has been shown by extensive studies in southern Africa and Malawi, and by a considerable body of African proverbs relating to bedbugs.[21]

At some stage in the 1980s bedbugs had reached a degree of rarity that formally qualified them for a place on the IUCN Red List of Threatened Species. Few people now recognized a bedbug when shown one: most believed that bedbugs are small, almost invisible animals that live in mattresses and confused them with dust mites. But who could blame ordinary, worried people when even control experts would come up with a veritable zoo of mistaken identities.

Since about 2000, however, and just before it was close to disappearing in the Western world, the bedbug has celebrated a fantastic comeback – in hostels and hotels of all classes, in the army barracks of several countries, in the musical *Bedbugs!!!* (2008), which had a successful run Off-Broadway in 2014, and in

Kenneth Mellanby, the founder of modern bedbug research in Britain. His field site was an animal room at the University of Sheffield, where rats were kept and where bedbugs roamed freely

Mistaken identity. This leaflet was issued by pest control authorities in the northwest of England. The picture shows a tick and may not particularly enforce public trust in pest authorities.

the involvement of the u.s. courts in tackling bedbugs, as in 1930s Berlin. Bedbugs now appear in children's books and crawl prominently through the Internet. Thousands of websites report experiences with bedbugs.

Data from Denmark has shown that the low-key trend had started almost unnoticed in the 1980s. Reports of bedbugs in the u.s., Australia and the United Kingdom increased only from the 1990s. The situation in other countries has been less clear, presumably the result of a lack of bedbug reports rather than their true absence. Most countries in the East and West, however, now recognize bedbugs as a growing current urban pest, from China to Chile, from Sweden to Switzerland, from Belgium to Brazil. Maps have been created, mainly in the u.s. but also worldwide, to which people can submit their bedbug sightings.

The Internet accelerates both awareness and fear, even though the benefits of increased awareness may be small because few people seem able to make the connection between a large bedbug depicted on a poster and the actual insect crawling in their surroundings.[22] The Internet also provides enough space and

Mistaken identity in a club in New York. Many kinds of vermin are easily classified as bedbugs: in this case, a cockroach.

38

A popular bingo game in Mexico, designed to 'play and learn' (*juega y aprende*). Bedbugs appear as females in their correct representation, but are translated as 'homemade bug' (and a rather funny suggestion for pronouncing it). A shield bug also appears as a 'bedbug'.

anonymity for people to seek advice, to point the finger at infested properties and hotels, and to pester other people at length with their bedbug experiences. Their appearances in fictional horror stories also aggravate the angst. Hundreds of photographs presenting all sorts of bare skin sporting real or supposed bedbug bites have been uploaded to dozens of websites, begging the empathy of the anonymous reader. In parallel, there has been a flood of cartoons, videos and blog discussions on the sex life of the bedbug that totally eclipse anything in *Fifty Shades of Grey* – indeed, the anonymity of the Web releases hidden desires.

What is this animal that people use as a facade, as a screen, to externalize their phobias, to present themselves in a certain way? How does it live and what does it do?

3 Bug Life

The word 'bedbug' describes the insect's favourite place, and the one that is most consistent over time and geographical location. This insect was all too obviously present in the Rome of Gaius Valerius Catullus (1st century BC).[1] Carl Linnaeus noted its preference when selecting its Latin name in 1758 (*lectus* meaning sofa or bed). Its very habitat served as indirect evidence for the presence of a bed in Springfield Town Hall in *The Simpsons*.

In most Indo-Germanic and Slavic languages the word for bedbug translates as wall-louse, such as the Swedish *vägglus*, or the Serbian *stenica*. Bedbugs, of course, occupy many other habitats. As thousands of pictures reveal, they have also been found on chairs, armchairs and wheelchairs, in beds and bedsits, in clothes and closets, in clocks and cots, in plugs and pinholes, in suits and suitcases, as well as in radios and radiators. Bedbugs were so common in radios that a scientific survey of household pests in Finland in 1974 used radio repair shops as an explicit source of inquiries, alongside local health authorities and local veterinary and agricultural authorities. The bedbugs' predilection for radios was probably caused by the tendency of the old transistor and valve models to heat up in use, thereby creating a snug and warm environment. A century earlier, when large floor-standing clocks were in fashion, the Berlin-based caricaturist Heinrich Zille (1858–1929) explained that big clocks that stopped working could be

Images of aggregated bedbugs in an infestation situation are still widely used today to illustrate articles about bedbugs. Note the dark patches in some individuals – guts half-filled with semi-digested blood shining through a rather translucent cuticle. The images of the male and female clearly show the pointy abdomen of the male as its characteristic feature.

repaired by brushing the bedbugs out with a goose feather.[2] A pamphlet published by the Natural History Museum in London is more detailed in its description of the living places of bugs, but still feels this is not exhaustive enough and sees the need to close the list with 'etc., etc.' Hence, one could easily think that other appropriate names for the bedbug would be radio bug, hot-water cylinder bug, back-of-the-picture bug, skirting board bug, wallpaper bug, sash-window box bug, upholstered-chair-and-settee bug, batten bug, behind-the-rose-of-electric-light-or-gas-fittings bug, or occasionally under-lavatory-seat bug, etc., etc. Electric plugs are still frequently mentioned today, whereas, like radios, hot-water cylinders have gone out of fashion.

Where there are bedbugs, especially when they have not been disturbed for quite some time, there are often many of them: 'In every pit and screwhole, every joint and crack they clustered, so thickly that sometimes there were whole marshalled lines of them',[3] or as the 'Bugg-Destroyer' Andrew Cooke (see Chapter

Two) asserted about a servant's bed, 'no beehive was ever fuller' and 'there wasn't a patch that wasn't crammed with them.' Indeed, bedbugs like to cuddle. When two of them are released in a small glass container with some paper, they will huddle against each other, even if wood is offered on the other side. Bedbugs like the rough surface of wood, but they prefer paper when there is someone to snuggle. Of course, the social behaviour of forming small groups does not work in the bedbug's favour. The phenomenon of sitting near another individual of your species in order to make bodily contact is called thigmotaxis, and the bedbug was the very animal in which such behaviour was first identified in 1932.[4] The phenomenon of thigmotaxis later became important when it was shown to cause migratory locusts to switch from the solitary to the swarming type.

For bedbugs to satisfy their desire to cuddle, they first have to find each other. What is it that brings bedbugs together, then keeps them together and makes them stay together? This is down to a chemical that scientists have named an 'aggregation pheromone'. Until recently we had no clue what this substance might be, but the initiated among us can smell bedbugs. Balzac was able to describe the bugs' smell as the typical odour of French boarding houses.[5] The writer Ruth Park describes how 'a faint filthy smell arose from them alive. Dead, they would smell overpoweringly, of mingled musk and ammonia.'[6] Some researchers, including myself, can even tell different colonies and different species from their smell. Scientific experiments have shown that even small amounts of bug faeces attract other bedbugs, thus causing their aggregation, and that such a smell is attractive for months.[7]

A different smell appears when bedbugs are squeezed or squashed, or when, as already mentioned, plant bugs are accidentally bitten while residing in raspberries. This sharp, piercing smell is the one that Martin Luther ascribed to his arch-enemy, Erasmus of Rotterdam, and what is now called the alarm pheromone. However, appearances can be deceiving and the two smells are not actually so different. It was not until 2015 that scientists in Canada settled the issue and identified which substances were attractive and which caused alarm responses. The sharp 'stink' alarm smell makes bugs run away when there is a lot of it, and it translates to 'danger around'. However, when there is a low level of this smell, it seems to indicate that the danger occurred a while ago, and the message now translates to 'other bugs are here'. And as bugs like other bugs, they get together – this is how the snuggling in bedbugs comes about.

One thing the ancestor bedbug needed to do, regardless of whether it lived on pigeon or bat, was to withstand long periods without their usual blood supply, which had migrated to warmer winter quarters. Bedbugs who couldn't cope without food for half a year or more came to a fatal end. The bugs that coped were the ones that are here today, and this is why they all have this marvellous survival ability. Bedbugs can starve – that is, not

The European swallow bug, *Cimex hirundinis*. This species, as shown here, lives and overwinters in the nests of house martins.

drink – for half a year, or perhaps for even longer. The cold helps them to survive periods of food shortage. The bugs adjust their bodily functions to a very low level, just sufficiently high for them to be able to switch back to their normal life machinery when conditions improve. This can be neatly seen in the bedbug's closest relative, the swallow bug. There can be dozens, hundreds or thousands of swallow bugs residing in a single swallow nest and feasting on the chicks, who suffer tremendously. In the autumn, however, the swallows migrate south, apparently never taking any of the bugs on their journey. When the swallows return in the spring, the swallow bugs become active again after they have patiently waited in switched-off mode for the return of the swallows.

The long period of starvation gives the bugs one of their most distinct characteristics: their flatness. During this time they digest everything they have consumed, completely emptying their gut, and any reserves become mobilized for use. Consequently, they become flat in shape and even as transparent as parchment, 'of zero thickness, so several dozens of them could sneak into any

Bedbugs are notorious for fitting into tiny spaces, even pinholes.

A hungry bedbug can be as flat as a piece of paper, as can be seen in this photograph. Also note the size of the egg just above the bug.

one of numerous small cracks in the bed'.[8] They are so flat that, as a British government report says, they can fit in a single nail hole. The descriptive German name *Tapetenflunder* (wallpaper flounder), particularly used in Berlin, denotes the flat-bodied nature of bedbugs, as does the North American Mahogany flats, the Dutch *platjes* and several other names.[9]

When flat, bedbugs can remain undetected for quite some time. This characteristic makes them an appropriate choice for the naming of secret surveillance devices, as is seen in the German *Wanzen*, the Italian *cimice*, the Chinese *qiètīngqì*, the Polish *pluskwa* or the Serbian *stenica*, all words referring to both bedbugs and surveillance bugs. It is also visible in the English expression 'to bug a room'. The history of the electronic bug is not entirely clear, but one of the first uses must have been the surveillance of the u.s. embassy in Moscow when one was hidden inside a wooden Great Seal presented by members of the Soviet Communist Children's Organization in 1945. What later became known as the Great Seal Bug did its service until it was discovered in 1952.[10] In remarkable contrast to the concealed microphones that are called 'bugs' in various local languages, the 'computer bug' is a global reference and remains in its English form in many languages.

Bedbugs leave their secret hiding place when they are hungry in order to search for food at night: 'As the darkness grew deeper the bugs came out of their cracks in the walls, from under the paper, and out of the cavities in the old iron bedsteads, where they hung by day in grape-like clusters.'[11] However, while 'the flat bug is more ravenous . . . even he will allow you time to go to sleep before he begins with you'.[12] The bug children in the Hopi tales are also warned by their parents: 'Don't approach a person right away. Wait until you're sure the person's fast asleep, then make your move.'[13] The nocturnal habit of bedbugs to search for food can be broken, though. After many years of feeding during day-light, bugs of laboratory colonies don't wait any longer till the person is fast asleep. The bugs' appetite can be elicited in even the

Rolf Staeck, caricature mocking a popular advertisement by a telephone company ('just call your friends'), playing on the double meaning of 'bugs' and 'Wanzen' as insects and electronic surveillance devices. The postcard was produced amid several scandals of illegal telephone surveillance by the German secret service in the 1980s.

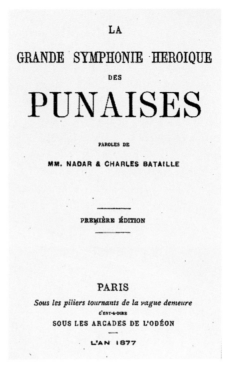

LA

GRANDE SYMPHONIE HEROIQUE

DES

PUNAISES

PAROLES DE

MM. NADAR & CHARLES BATAILLE

———
PREMIÈRE ÉDITION
———

PARIS

Sous les piliers tournants de la vague demeure
C'EST-A-DIRE
SOUS LES ARCADES DE L'ODÉON

L'AN 1877

brightest light by a single tapping of the colony box, inducing wild scuttling of bugs in anticipation of a meal.

Bedbugs that cannot get to their victim directly have often been asserted to crawl along the wall and ceiling to drop onto the sleeper's bed, a behaviour reported in Russia by Tolstoy. He later, however, claimed that he could feel a bedbug biting him, which cannot have been true, so undermining the factual accuracy of his work. Sheldon Lou claimed that bedbugs in China climbed up and 'parachuted down'.[14] In Nadar and Charles Bataille's *Grand Heroic Symphony of Bedbugs*, they drop in droves from the ceiling while others climb down. In Ben Winters's modern horror story *Bedbugs*, bugs 'began to fall, dropping in uneven, weightless rows to the kitchen floor, where they landed like paratroopers, scurrying off to the corners, alone, in pairs or little groups'.[15]

The alleged, or real, dropping of bedbugs from the ceiling has led to an adventurous interpretation of the Portuguese word for bedbug, *percevejo*. It has been suggested that *percevejo* represents a head-first or precipitate action, also described by the Latin words *praeceps* or *praecipitis*.[16] *Percevejo* also means barnacle, and anyone who has tried to pluck a bedbug or a barnacle off a surface will see the striking resemblance. Although hardly ever reported in the scientific literature, the parachuting behaviour of bedbugs is so commonly mentioned in fiction that there may be more truth in it than in other oft-repeated myths. But perhaps the metaphor is just too beautiful. One reason to doubt this behaviour, however, comes from the observation that bedbugs cannot smell, or see, their victim over long distances: current knowledge suggests that even half a metre is too far. Are bedbugs attracted by the sleeper's ascending warm breath? At least that would explain why two famous writers both had bedbugs fall into their hot drinks – milk for George Orwell, and coffee for Alfred Edmund Brehm.

Once bedbugs have reached a target, they drink. And drink. And drink – up to three times their own body weight: the ultimate binge-drinkers. Ruth Park described how 'before the dawn they would return to their foul hiding-places round and glistening and bloated with blood, so fat they could hardly waddle.'[17] Sometimes, as Clive Sinclair observes, they can even be 'too bloated to return to their hiding places'.[18]

The bedbugs' stealthy lifestyle of drinking blood and their habit of helping themselves uninvited to one's very own fluid are possibly the strongest psychological elicitors of fear that people have of bedbugs. The itching bites are physical: not at all pleasant,

The segmented bedbug. The bedbug consists of a head and ten discrete body segments. The last two and the first two segments are merged.

but usually bearable. But having one's own bodily juices withdrawn without consent is perhaps too much to be tolerable. And there may be more behind this aversion to unwillingly sharing one's blood. The female protagonist in Winters's *Bedbugs* observes how their feeding behaviour desecrated her motherly feelings towards breastfeeding, with her baby 'huffing at her breast . . . drawing the fluid free . . . Now *it* was feeding. The bug, this monster, was drinking of her, too.'[19]

Drinking three times their body weight makes the bedbug sluggish and slow, and a good swatting target for disturbed sleepers. It also fuels a vicious mating ritual, because the bloated female bedbug is defenceless against mating attempts by males. This doesn't sound vicious until you hear that, in order to mate, the male drives a penis 'knife' into her belly. (We will return to this behaviour in the next chapter.) Getting back to normal shape, bedbugs employ a super-diuretic body machinery: most of the blood's water content is expelled from the body within a few hours, and the bug is free to return to the finest, that is the thinnest, cracks.

Binge-drinking also requires something else: a very expandable body, or at least some very expandable parts. The strong and stiff cuticle plates covering the bedbug back and belly are connected by pieces of expandable skin of a special and very elastic material. The stiff segments are a typical feature of bedbugs, giving them their characteristic appearance and making them among the defining features of children's drawings of bedbugs. They are also the typical feature of bedbugs in most, if not all, cartoons and other representations. A video posted on YouTube explains that to draw a bedbug step by step, one needs to draw an oval, add two oval-shaped wing remainders on top, add legs and draw lines across the body to indicate the segments – and then, the bedbug is ready.

An expanded, 'armour-plated', 'dome-like brown . . . body with arched segments' is, of course, the insect that Gregor Samsa famously turned into one morning. Newer research suggests that the bedbug may have been Kafka's *Metamorphosis* model,[20] even though I found that references to cockroaches seem to be favoured by translators in several languages. While his 1912 novella

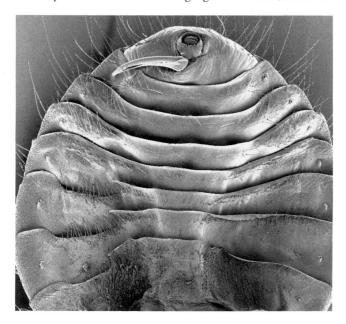

A scanning electron micrograph of the belly of a bedbug, in this case the African species *Afrocimex constrictus*, clearly showing the segmented body and, at the end of the abdomen, the copulatory knife, which in this species is rather blunt. The species has, therefore, featured as a sexual torturer in a novel by Bernard Werber.

One of only two artistic reliefs of bedbugs. This one is on the balcony of the London School of Hygiene and Tropical Medicine, along with a series of other blood-sucking or vector insects. Note the segmented body and the two remnants of wings that feature in many representations.

A child's drawing (Lina, six years old) of a bedbug, emphasizing the 'parasite brown' and the clear segmentation of the body.

originally had almost been named *The Bug*, it is not clear whether Kafka saw real bedbugs in front of him – the description in the text fits the bedbug well, but also that of many other insects. Some suggested that he might have copied passages from *Brehms Thierleben*, Germany's most famous encyclopaedia on animals, first published in 1864, with many later editions. I am unable to find any resemblance between the phrasing of Kafka's *Metamorphosis* and any of the editions of *Brehms Thierleben* prior to 1912. Instead, I find Brehm's text rather similar to extended passages of John Southall's *Treatise of Buggs* (1730). Strikingly, Brehm's 1869 edition also contains a description of a paint-splotched bedbug that crawls along a wall after it has been painted. This undoubtedly uncommon observation is almost identical to the earlier description by the Swiss author Gottfried Keller in one of the stories in his collection *Die Leute von Seldwyla* (The People of Seldwyla, 1856).[21] Such coincidences are not restricted to literature. It would be interesting to speculate why such plagiarism occurred – why was it worth the effort? Was it a status symbol back then, too, to write about the infamous bedbug?

A bedbug that is just about to finish its blood meal. The droplet at the end of the abdomen is usually expelled just before the end of feeding. The droplet consists of old blood and is the agent that leaves the well-known black spots on bedsheets that horrify so many people.

Just before they finish their blood meal, bedbugs release a drop of old, blackened blood that has been in their gut. It drops near where they feed – onto the sheets, or more specifically, onto *your* sheets. As Clive Sinclair writes in 'Bedbugs', they 'excrete their waste upon the sheets and make their getaway. When I awake I observe the tell-tale black stains.'[22] Releasing black, tell-tale drops on pure, immaculate sheets perfectly destroys the illusion that you are on your own in bed. Some have coldly calculated the loss in economic value of black-stained furniture, or even black-stained chicken eggs from the work of bedbugs. That may all be true, but these costs seem to be negligible when compared to the invasion of one's privacy, causing 'horrible torturing nightmares of bedbugs. They were marching across her stomach, leaving behind them a trail of that disgusting brown-black dust – *feces*,' as described by Ben Winters.[23] In this case, the psychology is correct but the biology is not: the faeces are dried liquid drops, not dust. The black spots, though, are a real reminder that you are not entirely in control. Most people have skin reactions to bedbug bites that are less intense than mosquito bites, and one could regard bedbugs lightly – especially when their numbers are low. However, taking bedbugs lightly is impossible when they leave marks on your bed – visible to you and your bed guests.

The nightmares caused by bedbugs have been described, one may almost say beautifully described, by the hard rock band Pearl Jam. In their song 'Bugs' (1994), the bugs are entering the singer's body via the head and ears, causing torment. He eventually gives up fighting them and resolves to become one with them, resulting in an amazing display of scratching and grating accordion sounds that perfectly portray the human fear of unwanted invasion and the enslaving of the body by bugs from the outside. It is very different from Kafka's escapist, attention-seeking and internally driven metamorphosis in the search for paternal emancipation.

Copper engraving in a children's book edited by Friedrich Justin Bertuch, showing a bedbug and stages of the corn moth, c. 1820. The bedbug apparently was later copied and appeared in an identical posture in other works, such as in Kielsen's *Icones insectorum* (1835).

Different shapes of faecal droplets. While appearing ridiculous at first sight, this research by Albrecht Hase was originally carried out to investigate whether the shape of the spots reveal something about the history of bedbugs in an infestation. This information would have been useful in court to decide whether previous or current tenants were to blame for the infestation of an apartment.

The scrambling, mincing and crushing sounds of an accordion may also represent the paranoid thoughts of someone who thinks they have parasites but who in fact does not. This medical condition is known as Ekbom syndrome and it can cause people to seriously harm themselves. Analysing the descriptions of people's bedbug fears posted on public websites reveals that many people show signs of suffering from symptoms of Ekbom syndrome or reacting as though, as Winters puts it, bedbugs 'feed on body and soul'.[24]

After bugs have soiled the sheets, they return home. In the Hopi stories they are greeted by their families, but in reality the bugs are welcomed by an evaporative chemical cocktail from defecating comrades in their refuges. Once back in their refuges, bedbugs do what they are here for – they reproduce, that is, they lay eggs. For a long time it was believed that after a night out, a bedbug would always return to the harbourage in which it had spent the day (the 'nest'). This belief was recently disproved for good by my colleague Richard Naylor in a single night. Richard built small artificial 'rooms', which were long (3 m) but quite narrow (20 cm). These had open tops to allow observation and could accommodate ten or more harbourages. Richard marked all the bedbugs sitting in each harbourage with a specific colour, and then provided food at one end of his 'room'. The bedbugs marched off to the food, of course, but did not return 'home': the next morning, bugs in the refuges showed a mix of different colours.

In the refuge, a fully fed female produces up to thirty eggs from one blood meal, that is approximately thirty eggs per five to ten

A small bedbug refuge developed to serve in laboratory research. The feeding source is at the viewer's end.

days. Needless to say, extremely large numbers could build up if females had the chance to dine regularly, and Sheldon Lou's assertion that bedbugs 'proliferated exponentially' would be proven correct. However, accruing a large number of bedbugs also increases the risk of bedbugs being detected and suffering the consequences from an unwilling host (see Chapter Seven).

It is the accumulation of these large numbers of bedbugs that creates a striking parallel to the electronic bugs detected in the telephones of the leaders of many Western countries throughout 2014 and 2015. Planted by other Western secret services, these electronic bugs were seemingly also able to reproduce out of control, exceeding anything one could have imagined even from George Orwell's 1949 novel *Nineteen Eighty-four*.

Not every bug is able to find food or return to a refuge, and as such they can go astray – getting lost and ending up in somebody's clothes, suitcase, plush toy, car or other belonging – just as their cousins are sometimes accidentally transported on bat wings or swallow feet.

Usually the bug is alone when it goes astray. Establishing a new family is, then, an enterprise that will not work if the lost, lonely bug is a male, unless he meets a resident female in an existing infestation, of course. Currently, infestation rates in the West have not reached the levels observed in the 1930s, so chances are high that bugs arriving at a new place will now meet an empty space. Empty of bugs, that is. The chances of setting up a family are better if the lost singleton is a female, but she needs to have been fertilized before she got lost. We do not know how often newly arriving single females succeed in founding new families, or in other words, cause an infestation, and how many fail. But what we do know is that most house infestations consist of one family founded by a single fertilized female. We can tell that from the similarity of the genes carried by the infesting individuals.[25] Inside the female, the sperm will last approximately eight weeks.[26] With a regular food supply, that is sufficient to found a family of two hundred. The offspring from the first batch of laid eggs will have grown up after eight weeks and the female can receive a new supply of sperm from her own sons. The sons can also mate with their sisters, and this helps to expand the family and create close genetic ties. Surprisingly, this incestuous Oedipus scenario has not appeared in any bedside horror book or any work of fiction. I am waiting for this to happen, unless something about this is too horrific even for horror writers. Anyhow, now it is high time to call a pest controller, and we will follow him (yes, him!) in Chapters Seven and Eight. But before that we look into the bedbug's sex life.

A myth destroyed. A bedbug refuge showing differently painted bedbugs. All bugs from one refuge were painted with the same colour. Then food was offered and the homing of bedbugs recorded. As this photograph shows clearly, bedbugs from at least five different refuges had gathered into a new community made up of bugs from the originally green, green-yellow, yellow, yellow-red and red-green-yellow refuges. This disproved the theory that individual bedbugs return to the same spot.

4 Bug Sex: Real and in Fiction

Tainting bedsheets and thereby erecting a flag of ownership in foreign territories does not exactly serve to make many friends. However, matters may get worse when the sheet owners realize just what outrageous and gruesome sex practices are performed in their bed. The bizarre sex lives of bedbugs has been widely covered in the media, a fact that not every animal can claim. Moreover, the headlines, blog entries, cartoons and even videos that interpret the results of bedbug sex research have iconized sexual machismo and sparked a debate about the representation of scientific results in the popular press. They have also been used as examples to argue that behaviours such as homosexuality or sadomasochistic practices are found in the animal kingdom, and hence are normally occurring in wider nature – whoever might need such justification. So, what is it about the sex life of the bedbug that sparks such exaggerated and diverse responses?

To put it mildly, bedbugs have an unusual mode of reproduction. To begin with, bedbug males do not court females, but just pounce upon them. Once sitting on the female, the male does not, like in most other animals, insert his copulatory organ into the female genital opening. The male does it in a different way: the male's copulatory organ, which looks like a knife, is stabbed through the skin into the female's belly.[1] On closer inspection, the male's organ rather resembles an injection needle through which,

Stevyn Colgan's cartoon seriously explaining an aspect of the reproductive biology of bedbugs while using a funny method to emphasize the sharpness of the male penis. The knife is secured by a cork.

after it has been inserted into the female, the male directs the fluids directly into the female. Sperm are deposited more or less into the female's bodily fluid. They then travel by their own propulsion through the female body, perhaps following areas with the highest concentration of oxygen. Once the sperm have reached the tube through which the eggs are transported downwards (the oviduct), they somehow get through the tissue of the oviduct and move upwards towards the ovary and towards the eggs, a journey not without its dangers. While the sperm cells are waiting to find entry into the oviduct, they may be attacked by bacteria and other germs that resided on the male's copulatory needle and were transferred during mating. Sperm that have survived this exciting, and probably exhausting, route do something that again happens in very few other animals: they fertilize the eggs while they are still in the ovary – a kind of pre-ovulation conception.

Some of this sounds quite dramatic for the female, especially the stabbing through the belly, which is formally known as traumatic insemination.[2] And it is. How do females survive it? The somewhat counter-intuitive answer is that females survive because most of their ancestors died; in other words, only females that had survived the deadly male attacks in the past were able to produce offspring, with this survival ability written in their genes. Those females produced more offspring, which themselves laid more eggs after surviving the sexual procedure. Over time the only females that remained were those that were best at surviving traumatic insemination and laying eggs – natural selection.

DISCOVERING THE BEDBUG'S MATING HABITS: HUNTS FOR FAME

The first details of traumatic insemination, uncovered by the British entomologists W. S. Patton and F. W. Cragg, were presented in their 1913 textbook, *A Textbook of Medical Entomology*.

This was preceded by long disputes between several discoverers of different female organs of bedbugs, or any of their parts, and how precisely, and in what direction, the sperm would move through the female body. In 1918 the German zoologist Albrecht Hase published a paper on copulation in bedbugs, suggesting that he was the first to discover it. Perplexingly, Hase never mentioned any of Patton and Cragg's observations, a point of neglect that was not taken kindly by Robert Usinger and which he explicitly pointed out in the 1966 *Monograph of Cimicidae*. Usinger never sought cheap recognition and rarely criticized other people's work openly, but he very much respected priority. In addition, Patton and Cragg's description of the bedbug's mating ritual, which they twice laid out at length in their book, is a much better account than Hase's, because they had dissected females after mating to confirm that sperm were actually transferred. Was it war-related confusion by the usually encyclopaedic Hase that had let him conclude that he was the first and that Patton and Cragg's treatment was superficial? We may never know, nor whether it was also coincidental that the next exhaustive examination of the bedbug to follow in German, by Heinrich Kemper in 1936, also neglected to mention Patton and Cragg's work.

Some fifty years later there was another race involving bedbug sex. Different species of bedbugs have dramatically different female sex organs, ranging from a complete absence, to a complicated tube system, to a full duplication of the organ on both sides of the body. The order in which one step evolved from another was a matter of much disagreement. This time the players were both influential entomologists of their time: Jacques Carayon, operating from the trench of his histology and microscopy laboratory in Paris, and Howard Everest Hinton, who disputed from his desk and library at the University of Bristol. Without going into too much detail, these two researchers never solved the question of whether or not normal copulation, which occasionally wounds the female, preceded traumatic insemination. Indeed it largely remains a mystery today.

There must have been something about fame and bedbug sex, because forty years later another bedbug research race ensued. In 2001 scientists calculated the price of defence in the female bedbug. Having sex four times a week was enforced by the male bedbugs, which ultimately led to the death of the females after 110 days, compared to the 150 days that females would have lived if they mated at their own pace, once every month. However, even the 110 days survival required females to invest energy and pay the price for the maintenance of a special organ that defends against traumatic insemination. This organ is called the spermalege. However, against what exactly does the female organ defend? This seemed an obvious question, at least to the initiated, and it occurred to two bedbug researchers simultaneously: Professor Göran Arnqvist at Uppsala University, and Professor Michael Siva-Jothy at the University of Sheffield. Each of them hired a scientist to help answer this question of defence. An Englishman, Dr Ted Morrow, was hired in Sweden, the other in England – me. It was not so much of a competition as the previous bedbug races, because both research groups were unaware of each other's work. Eventually, both research groups submitted their work to the same Royal Society journal, where both articles were peer-reviewed together and both appeared in the same issue of the journal, next to each other.[3] The methods were pretty much identical, which is not surprising as the research question was so specific. However, the results differed starkly. One research group found that the female organ defended against the bodily damage incurred from sex, whereas the other group found that the special female organ defended against sexually transmitted microbes. The only thing that differed between the research groups was that in one laboratory the females generally lived for much longer. I was lucky to be able to continue with the research, but it was not for another twelve years after collaborating with colleagues that I was able to show that both results were actually correct, despite their contradictory nature.

For a change, the latest race for bedbug fame was not about bedbug sex, and again ended in a draw. This was the hunt to decipher the bedbug's genome. The human genome project, which back then had cost millions of u.s. dollars, pounds sterling, Deutschmarks and francs, was accomplished in 2001. The work was driven by competition between two groups: an American private company and a publicly funded global network of universities and research institutions. Both groups ended up working on slightly complementary parts of the genome but finished at almost the same time. Today, we can sequence the entire DNA make-up of an individual human in an afternoon, give or take a few hours. The genomes of more than 70,000 organisms have been sequenced, but for some time this did not include the bedbug. In 2010 researchers from various laboratories joined ranks to collaborate on a cheaper method to sequence the bedbug genome. The collaborative sequencing of the bedbug genome was completed in 2012, after which the endless arrangement of the four letters of DNA – A, G, T, C – had to be interpreted into gene functions. On their own, these letters are meaningless. In this case there were 650 million letters to interpret. This meant combing through the letters to look for the start and end of a specific gene before ticking it off as complete. In the case of the bedbug, 14,000 ticks were made. Dozens of groups were involved, each specialized in their field. Can you get any more specialist than bedbug DNA, you may ask? Yes, you can. For example, one can work on identifying genes that are only associated with bloodsucking, or digestion, or mating, or whatever. Know thy gene and you will get the chance to go through the DNA letters of the bedbug genome – in fact, more than 36 research groups did. After the research groups had finished identifying the genes, they had to comb through the genome again. This time they needed to compare it with the genomes of other insects, such as the famous fruit fly and the pea aphid, the closest relative to the bedbug that had then been sequenced. This comparison allowed the researchers to see which genes were different, additional or missing in the bedbug. Everyone wants to get rid of bedbugs (except me, of course) and therefore looking at the genome of the bedbug can help in the design of pesticides to achieve this. There seems much reputable gain in conducting genomic research into the bedbug, but there is also much to lose if you are not the first there, because silver medallists rarely become famous. It is a challenge because DNA sequence analysis methods develop rapidly and become cheaper by the day, and different research groups may join forces to sequence the genome or come up with a quicker, automated way of identifying genes. In fact, this is exactly what happened. Suddenly and unexpectedly, a second group, mostly newcomers to the field with little connection to established bedbug researchers or to the other bedbug genome group, sequenced the bedbug genome. This second group looked beyond adult bedbugs, as well as comparing the genomes of fed and starved bedbugs, to increase their chances of finding active genes. While reporting a similar 14,000 identified genes for the adult bedbug, the newcomers also reported 36,000 identified genes for the entire species, which was more genomic information than had been collected for any sequenced insect to date. The newcomers were also faster in submitting their findings to a journal, driving the first team as well to finish and submit their results quickly. The results by the 'first' group of bedbug researchers, however, were more readily accepted by the peer reviewers, but then the manuscript laid on the publisher's desk for months.

At last the two research groups agreed to wait and have their research articles published next to each other in the journal. This orchestrated pretence of harmony was the eventual outcome. A race for fame to decipher a genome had not happened since the race for the human genome, so the bedbug should feel honoured. In the case of the human genome, there had been concerns that the private funding company would monopolize the genomic sequences for their own research, fuelling the other group's determination to make the results public. However, such noble concerns had not sparked the race in bedbugs.

ANTAGONISTIC BUSINESS

The traumatic mating of bedbugs is a highly informative example of the antagonism between males and females, also known as sexual conflict, or the battle of the sexes. This and other conflicts are known to propel evolution and, as a result, bedbugs have become a model system in evolution research. The rapid evolution comes about because females must have responded quickly to the traumatic mating, otherwise they would be extinct today. In theory, females have three ways to respond: first, they could avoid most matings by simply running away from males. Or, second, they may possess something – an organ, a specific behaviour, anything really – that injures the male upon their attacks and so forces males to think twice about another belly-stabbing. As a third possibility, females might persevere throughout the gruesome sex and repair the damage afterwards. By the way, this trinity represents the general codex of how to solve conflicts: avoidance, fighting back (resistance) or toleration. We will later see whether these responses are useful for humans to deal with bedbugs (see Chapter Nine).

Females cannot respond in the first way described above, which is to avoid mating, because they are caught in a trap: only

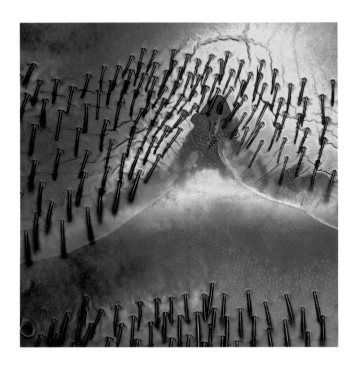

females that have not fed are parchment-flat and so able to press their body to the ground, thereby concealing the belly from the males' attempts. Abstaining from feeding to keep the belly flat is, however, not possible, because females who don't feed will not leave any offspring or grandchildren, meaning that such females would not exist today. Females that do feed have a bloated body that cannot be pressed to the ground. This leaves the male's favourite target, the female belly, exposed.

What about fighting back? Yes, females fight back against one aspect of the male's traumatic mating: on the inside of their bellies, an organ has evolved that gobbles up the microbes that the male brings in through mating. This was an exciting finding, because it was the first proper immune organ found in insects. This organ, however, strictly does nothing to fight males, only their microbes. Obviously males would not care too much about whether the female gobbles up the bacteria they have sexually transmitted to her.

The last possibility for females is to stand the pain and do something to ease it. In the spermalage described earlier, a special structure exists at the body site where the female is usually stabbed by the male, a deeply grooved and notched arrangement so that a randomly stabbing male would see its penis slide towards the end of the notch. Underneath this groove in the skin there is an elastic rubbery material – really soft, really elastic and really beautiful. This soft material makes it easier for the male to penetrate the female skin (yes, scientists actually measured the penetration force) and the easier the penetration, the less tissue damage to the female. The material built into the female stabbing site is called resilin. It is the most elastic material on the planet. It also has another effect that helps the female during traumatic insemination, but again leaves the male unharmed: it seals the female skin quickly and, therefore, prevents her from bleeding dry after sex.[4] If that is not enough to pique your interest, read on.

In a range of insects, the seminal fluid that the male transfers to the female alongside the sperm can be toxic to the sperm of other males, as well as toxic to females. However, the bedbug again proves the exception. In bedbugs, the semen instead contains an antibiotic, antioxidants and other goodies. In the laboratory, when the antibiotic substance of the semen was separately injected into bedbug females, females laid more eggs and – fountain of youth – they showed signs of ageing at a later stage in life.

Another aesthetic picture of the bedbug. In this case, it is the female organ that has to accommodate the copulatory knife. Scientists have found out that the blue-coloured patch comes from a very elastic material called resilin, which makes it easier for the female to survive the penetration of the skin by the male.

The intense research into the sexual organs of female bedbugs by Jacques Carayon in the 1950s and '60s was based on the study of hundreds of bedbugs, or of thinly sliced pieces of them. Studying the anatomy of their reproductive tracts to distinguish different species was all the fashion: Carayon found that many of the then eighty or so known bedbug species were almost indistinguishable from the outside, but looked very dissimilar in terms of their internal reproductive organs. He then revealed how these organs functioned, such as how the sperm are attacked by female immune cells inside the female. These complicated scientific details do not exactly sound like the material from which one

In French novelist Bernard Werber's classic novel of an ant state, *The Day of the Ants* (1992), victims are tortured by traumatic insemination from bugs. In the novel, which has not seen an English translation, actual scientific results – that sperm travel through the female body, that sperm are destroyed by female immune cells, and that female bedbugs invented a set of extra genitalia to cope with traumatic mating attempts – are bizarrely distorted and exaggerated. It is a work of fiction, and the reader will not be aware of what is true and what is invention.

would make a novel, yet Bernard Werber, a young French writer, did just that. His *Le Jour des fourmis* (The Day of the Ants), published in 1992, became a science-fiction classic. Embedded in the novel is a so-called 'Encyclopaedia of Relative and Absolute Knowledge', in which Werber creates a richly fantastic mixture of scientific facts, exaggeration and complete invention: for example, he describes traumatic insemination as occurring in gruesome sexual torture chambers.

One of the species that Carayon studied, and that Werber included in his book even with its Latin name, was *Afrocimex constrictus*. This bug occurs in caves that are teeming with thousands of Egyptian fruit bats. One of the caves has also been popularized by a BBC documentary showing that elephants mine the salty clay soil inside the cave. The idea of thousands of bats in a cave with elephants visiting sporadically to break a salty snack off the wall sounds like good material for a novel. Werber, however, preferred the bugs, for a good reason. While *Afrocimex constrictus* males do what all bedbugs do, drilling a hole into the skin of females in order to mate (so, nothing special here), they also pierce other males. They consequently transfer sperm to other males, which is one of the few cases of this happening in the entire animal kingdom. Amazingly, the usual female bedbugs' special organ, which evolved to cope with traumatic insemination, is also present in *Afrocimex* males but in no males of any other bedbug species. In *Le Jour des fourmis* the homosexual mating habits of *Afrocimex* torture renegade ants in a special torture chamber. The descriptions are quite explicit and Werber's treatment of the bedbugs is amazing due to the exaggeration and bizarre descriptions, rather than because it is beautifully written. The creation of beautiful prose was Clive Sinclair's achievement, just a few years before Werber.

The opening of Sinclair's 1982 short story 'Bedbugs' is not only the first account of the bizarre mating habits of the bedbug in

A collection of
short stories by
author Clive
Sinclair, including
'Bedbugs'. The
frontispiece
connects bedbugs
and the strange.

fiction, but it features a beautiful, if (naturally) drastic description
of what happens: 'A concrescence of male and female. The polluted
mass pulsates, masculine organs pullulate, grow into dangerous
spikes that, blinded by passion, miss the proffered orifices and
stab deep into the soft bellies of their consorts.'[5] The story goes
on to produce the ultimate cultural bedbug: a conglomerate of
blinded passion and gruesome stabbings and of blood-sucking,
faecal spots included. And bedbugs become both the witness and
the evidence of betrayal and of bizarre unions between Jewish
people – considered verminous bugs in the Third Reich – and
Germans.

Except for Carayon's work in the 1960s and the two texts we have just visited, things went a bit quiet for bedbugs and their sex life. This only changed, but dramatically so, around 2000, when the race to uncover the battle of the sexes described above took off, with interesting results.

The battle of the sexes is interesting material for journalists, and so it happened that a bright spotlight was shone on the bedbug. The sex practices of the bedbug have attracted such wide attention in the popular press that hundreds of newspaper articles, cartoons and blogs, even dramas on stage, exist on the topic. Many of them make rather predictable jokes with hardly veiled machismo.

Others are funnier or caricature the machismo. Yet others are gripping because of their beautiful presentation or imaginative

This cartoon by Paul Scott, 'Propagate', 23 February 2010, is an example of popular art representing the ambivalent atmosphere of biology and machismo surrounding the issue of traumatic mating in bedbugs.

treatment of the topic; and sometimes the imaginations of bloggers and cartoonists have gone wild. An interesting parallel of such sensationalism was noted within science journalism. The field as a whole, as well as some individual scientists and science writers, was accused of presenting the topic in an exaggerated sense: too sexy, as it were. For example, we presented our own findings under the heading 'bizarre gender-bender' after we found that some female *Afrocimex constrictus* (the ones described by Bernard Werber) possessed the male-type defence organs (which, as you may recall, the males had 'borrowed' from females in the first place). Females with those male-like organs also received fewer traumatic inseminations, causing a journalist to suggest the headline 'Bugs turn transsexual to avoid stabbing penises'.[6] This was criticized in the respected journal *Nature* as being anthropomorphic and sensationalist.[7] In this case, *Nature* unusually allowed the journalist to reply to the accusation and defend his view. (This only appears unusual when you know that *Nature* rarely allows corrections and responses, perhaps because it regards itself as infallible and assumes that responses are admissions that something had not been correct in the first place.) It is true that being 'transsexual' is more than an extra set of genitals and that the bugs do not possess these extra genitalia in order to prospectively avoid stabbings. Rather, these extra genital organs arose because it was advantageous to the female's ancestors. Given the need for brevity, however, I thought that the journalist's attention-gripping headline was, in effect, what happened. But I am no neutral observer and, in any case, I have seen worse distortions by the press. It was good to see the humble bedbug again involved in a little dispute.

One of the best-known videos on traumatic sex in bedbugs is that by Isabella Rossellini in her video series *Seduce Me* (2010).[8] A male can be seen approaching in the form of a knife, and we now know why. The female, rather aroused, cries directly into the camera, 'Chase Me! Mate with Me! Seduce me!' When stabbed by the male's copulatory knife, she looks anything but hurt. Her look becomes lustful when she explains that the sperm travel on their own to her ovaries. The touch of the forbidden makes bedbugs a perfect projection of the thrill that unusual sexual practices may give to their practitioners, while assuring the thrilled that some sexual practices and fantasies are not reprehensible, but occur quite naturally in nature.

Neither the fantasies nor their representations are a product of modern times alone, even though they had never reached today's numbers. The unwanted intimacy with bedbugs, perhaps coupled with the natural tendency to sleep naked in bed, may mix together feelings of horror, disgust and fear with an element of eroticism. Rather irrationally, and certainly medically incorrectly, bedbugs have been feared to enter human private orifices. The fear of allowing the outside world, exemplified by bedbugs, to physically connect to our inside is widespread across the globe. For example, in Aristophanes' *The Clouds*, Strepsiades likens the Corinthians to bugs, saying 'they are digging into my arse'. More beautifully and subtly phrased is a song from the Bahamas issued on an album by Maureen Duvalier (Calypso Mama) in 1957, all about a clever bedbug hiding in 'Muriel's Treasure'. The bedbugs in the village of the Hopi were clever in a similar way, although it is likely that the bedbug molesting the Hopi was of a different species.[9] In the Hopi folk tales the sexual connotation is strongest: here the bedbugs' lifestyle of sucking blood from the women's *löwas* (female genitalia) merges with promiscuous sexual activities and elicits male jealousy.[10] In the 1930s Kurt Tucholsky used four types of bugs to describe satirically the political and economic state of Germany. One of the bugs, the lustful one, is implied to enter a corpulent girl's treasure. Mirroring Tucholsky's association of bedbugs with a chubby ('and therefore kind') girl, in 'Reincarnation' the Trinidadian singer Rupert Westmore Grant (aka Lord Invader) also describes his desire to return as a bedbug, as he wants to bite young girls' buttocks, but he only wants to bite big women (after all, men are too hairy and their legs are too hard). Miss Sheily in Ruth Park's novel *The Harp in the South* threw infested furniture into the fire, saying, 'I'm sick of having my bottom nipped every time I sit on them', a situation mirrored by this anonymous English skipping rhyme:

The Bedbugs' Night Dance and Other Hopi Tales of Sexual Encounter

Collected, translated, and edited by Ekkehart Malotki
Introduction by E. N. Genovese

A collection of Hopi tales, two of them featuring bedbugs, or *pesets'ola*, in a very prominent way. These tales are the only hints of bedbugs being present before the arrival of the European settlers in America. Biological facts presented in the tales were later used to argue that the Hopi bedbugs may, in fact, refer to a different species parasitizing chickens and birds of prey.

Rupert Westmore Grant, aka Lord Invader, has a bedbug song in his repertoire, which states how he would like to be resurrected as a bedbug in order to bite certain ladies' bottoms.

A bug and flea
went out to sea
upon a reel of cotton.
The flea was drowned
But the bug was found
Biting a lady's bottom.[11]

Finally, in a more indirect way of relating bedbugs to entering body orifices, the Portuguese Jewish doctor Zacuto Lusitanus (1575–1642) is said to have recommended powdered bedbugs to somebody who had involuntarily granted a leech admission to his anal opening during a bath.[12] Does this remedy have an element of homeopathy ('same cures same'), as bedbugs were perceived as the archetypal body-enterer?

Entering other body orifices was apparently much less frequently mentioned. Just why bedbugs became associated with sexual activity even before details of their sex life were known will have to be left to speculation. It is not impossible that the Hopi, whose bugs sucked the *löwas* of girls and women, the people in the Caribbean who made Calypso Mama sing about 'Muriel's Treasure', or the Berliners who inspired Tucholsky to write about a bedbug seeking the same refuge mentioned by Calypso Mama, had all seen bedbugs copulating, which is what they do frequently, and thereby ascribed them the sexual connotation they now have.

This chapter will conclude with an example of how fiction attempted to creep into popular science. The German weekly

Poster exploiting the sexual connotation of the intimacy of bedbugs, the bed and the sleeper.

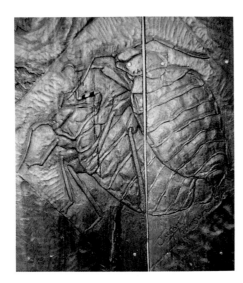

Jason Thompson, detail of *Oaken Evolution: The Darwin Panels*, installed in the Department of Animal and Plant Sciences, University of Sheffield, in 1998. The wood carving shows a mating pair of bedbugs, alongside (not visible) Darwin, *Archaeopteryx*, a skull and a brain. This representation proved to be visionary: a few years later, the bedbug had acquired the status of a significant model system in evolutionary biology. The entire artwork consists of seven panels measuring 2 m x c. 50 cm. The Department of Animal and Plant Sciences contributed important bedbug research in the 1930s and from the year 2000.

magazine *Focus*, when reporting about the newly discovered bio-material resilin in female bedbugs, directly linked it to human sexuality. But not only that, they also reported as fact that male bedbugs can mate 200 times a day – the very number Bernard Werber had ascribed to them in his 'Encyclopaedia of Relative and Absolute Knowledge', rather than the scientifically correct five times. It seems that this science journalist was more versed in fiction than in science.

On the catwalk of evolution, the bedbug became an important model for conflicts by entering the realm of fiction with its most private business. I am eager to see when, and how, more biological facts entered the fictional sphere and vice versa.

5 Itching to Succeed

If one closely watches a bedbug on the skin, one can observe how the tip of the proboscis is inserted, withdrawn, inserted again, and so forth – a sequence known as probing. Sometimes the entire head and forebody move up and down in the process, resulting in what is described as a 'rocking motion'. While rocking, the stylet is driven into the skin until a suitable blood vessel is found. Blood is then withdrawn during the next ten to fifteen minutes.

This bedbug habit of pricking the skin caused many languages to adopt the word bedbug as a moniker for a drawing pin or thumbtack, notably the French *punaise*, the Italian *cimice*, the Spanish *chinche*, or the Portuguese *percevejo* in Brazil. As graphic as this comparison is, it is not quite right biologically because the proboscis consists of two mouthparts, each consisting of a further two parts. One pair, called the mandibles, forms the outer tube of the proboscis, and the other pair, called the maxillae, forms the inner tube. This information, now the standard description of the bedbug proboscis in morphology textbooks for biology students, was only revealed under somewhat acute competition. The first extensive description of the bedbug proboscis was provided by Leonard Landois in 1869. The 1913 textbook by Patton and Cragg (see Chapter Four), which was also the first medical entomology textbook, shows a correct cross-section of the bedbug's sucking

Humorous postcards about bedbugs were plentiful in the early years of the last century. This one plays on the term 'big bugs' for famous people. Remarkably, a metal bed is depicted. Metal beds were assumed for many years, even centuries, to provide protection from bedbugs.

A bedbug sucking blood.

tube. Patton and Cragg, however, hardly mentioned Landois's previous work and provided fewer details than he did. In the following year C. Hay Murray 'gave the first correct interpretation' of the mouthpart structure but 'wrongly calls them [the inner pairs of stylets] the mandibles, and . . . does not mention the salivary channel', as I. M. Puri concluded in 1924.[1] The mistake of describing what are actually the maxillae as 'mandibles' was severely punished: these were hard times for the early anatomists. Puri also commented on the hooks on the inner tube of the bedbug proboscis, and noted that it is actually only the right maxilla that is inserted into the blood vessel. So, bedbugs are right-handed in some respect. I wonder how many more bites will have to be studied to reveal left-handers.

In 1929 Heinrich Kemper described the bedbug's act of piercing and sucking in extraordinary detail, especially the driving of the stylet into the skin by means of a forward and backward extension of the stylet, a little like a telescope. This observation was confirmed thirty years later, but with rather moderate credit to Kemper, by Dickerson and Michel Marie-Joseph Lavoipierre, who established that the stylet moves through the skin until it hits an actual blood vessel. Today, researchers equip the blood pump of bedbugs with electrodes to measure how often the bug's proboscis makes skin contact, how often the stylet is moved up and down, and how much blood is withdrawn and under which circumstances. The complicated technical descriptions by the anatomists of which mouthpart does what have now acquired a comical air and, while being presented as public performances on bedbugs by the German duo PariaCreation, they now serve a new purpose.

Despite near-ubiquitous claims to the contrary, a bite from a bedbug usually goes unnoticed by the victim. To remain undetected during feeding, it was seemingly advantageous for early bedbugs to use a painkiller or local anaesthetic on their host. This local anaesthetic is delivered through that tiny salivary canal, which is separate from the blood canal, and which had sparked controversy among early anatomists. The blood flow is maintained

Postcard from the early 1900s.

by an anti-coagulant, which prevents the clogging of the bug's proboscis. Finally, bedbugs also spit a chemical into the blood vessel to widen the vessel walls in order to extract as much blood in as little time as possible, so the time spent on the host is short. This cocktail of chemicals is what causes the itching later. I do not mean a psychological itch resulting from reading about these substances, but an actual itch after a bite.

Most of this information was again revealed under circumstances of competitive research. For example, Puri examined the salivary glands, which produce the three substances injected during a bedbug bite. He mistakenly credited the first description of the bedbug salivary glands to Landois, when in actual fact a beautiful, detailed and correct representation of the glands had already been given by Léon Jean-Marie Dufour in 1833. Despite this, the researchers were in agreement that there was one pair of round glands and one pair of pear-shaped glands. Puri gave additional credit to Murray, saying he 'for the first time traces the second duct of the large glands and shows that, after running forward for a short distance, it bends round, runs backwards and ultimately opens into the small salivary gland of its own side'. With this kind of bending prose it seems a minor miracle that the old anatomists understood each other at all, especially if translated into a different language. Puri went on: 'with a sharp razor a slice was cut off each side of the head and prothorax, holding the bug between thumb and forefinger' in order to extract 'twenty-five of the large and an equal number of the small glands'.[2] Mixing the contents of the respective glands with fresh human blood, he observed that the blood coagulated within twenty to thirty minutes upon mixing with the contents of the small gland; this was not any faster than the natural coagulation rate for blood left alone. However, when he mixed fresh human blood with the contents of the large gland, the blood did not coagulate in the course of 24 hours – a significant victory for Puri in the quest for novel discovery. But that was not all, he wanted to learn more.

> By pricking my forearm with a sterilized needle, on the point of which was the crushed salivary gland of a bedbug, and trying each pair of glands separately, I found that either of them produces a similar irritation to that felt after the bite of a bed-bug. In both cases the lesion could be seen for a fortnight, while when the prick was made with a clean sterilized needle, nothing was visible after the second or third day.[3]

Despite this detailed work, neither Heinrich Kemper nor Otto Hecht in the 1930s mentioned Puri's study (needless to say, Usinger did in 1966). Kemper and Hecht each aimed to tackle another problem and get their piece of the research cake. Kemper allowed a bedbug to bite him eighteen times, but without ever withdrawing blood. He developed eighteen welts, each of a similar size, thereby showing that saliva was injected before blood was taken. He also calculated how much saliva was injected. Otto Hecht was interested in something else. It was known that some people were insensitive (often called 'immune') to bedbug bites. The most famous and oft-repeated case is that of the biologist and geneticist J.B.S. Haldane. He was the first to bring genetics into bedbug research by stating that neither he nor his father responded to bedbug bites, implying that insensitivity to such bites was inherited. Otto Hecht worked with volunteers, including himself, to answer the question of inherent sensitivity to bites. He extracted blood serum from volunteers who were sensitive to bedbug bites and transplanted it into insensitive individuals, and vice versa. He then placed bugs on the site where he had injected the serum and recorded the volunteers' response. These experiments showing that insensitive people can become locally sensitive to bedbug bites, but not the other way round, have been largely neglected. Even if they were more widely acknowledged today, however, such experiments would probably be approached with great caution given the ethical concerns surrounding such crude transplants.

Pehr Kalm reported in 1748 that the French and English settlers in Canada suffered from bedbug bites, whereas the natives were not sensitive to bites. Conversely Carayon, travelling through western Africa, mentioned that the natives were bitten by *Leptocimex* but Europeans were not. Other broad but unproven, or simply wrong, generalizations about groups of people have also been made. Sheldon Lou described how a student from the countryside, unlike all of his roommates from Beijing, did not suffer from bites (and was therefore voted by the group to occupy the most bug-afflicted bed in the room). We will see in Chapter Eight that people singled out in some connection with bedbugs are often from a different social class, country or religion than the accusers. In fact, given the available scientific evidence, any conclusions about responses to bites by certain groups of people are outright ridiculous.

From 1929 to the present day medical entomology textbooks have stated that one person in five is insensitive to bedbug bites. This bold statement comes from a single study concerning one group of Europeans, probably all Germans. Heinrich Kemper from Berlin led this study in 1929 and observed 45 people for a few days after they had been bitten by bedbugs in a controlled experiment. Eight out of the 45 people showed no response to the bites, roughly 20 per cent, or one in five – the origin of the textbook statement. By subsequent, frequent repetition this number seems to have turned into truth. To be fair, Kemper's findings were reinforced in a 1985 study by a seemingly very precise recording of '21.43 per cent' of people that did not respond. Giving two decimal places suggests a large number of people were examined, but in fact, 21.43 per cent represented three persons out of fourteen.[4] Regardless, neither these nor subsequent studies monitored volunteers for more than a few days after the experimental bedbug bites. It was revealed after Kemper's study that the itchy red welts from bedbug bites may not occur until up to eleven days after the bite. Despite this information, nobody went back to repeat the sensitivity experiments over a duration of eleven days. It was easier to stick with the existing story: this is why the one-in-five 'fact' persisted.

When I found out about the origin of this textbook figure, it bugged me and I decided to enter the bedbug bite research race, even as a latecomer. In our laboratory in Sheffield we sometimes fed the bedbugs on ourselves, some of us repeatedly. This resulted in a small group of nineteen people whose skin reactions could be scored over several rounds of bites. Receiving their supposed first bite, the researchers did not show any skin reaction. Upon the second round of feeding, marks appeared eight to eleven days later, then two to five days after the third round of feeding, and more rapidly after that. Some who had been bitten dozens of times immediately showed red welts on the skin. Eventually only one out of the nineteen individuals who were repeatedly bitten remained unresponsive to bedbug bites – much fewer than 'one in five'. Nineteen is still not an impressive number on which to base a textbook figure and it needs to be re-examined by others. This may not happen, however, as the ethical guidelines for research change continuously: the paperwork necessary to repeat such a study would probably require an amount of time and energy that few researchers are prepared to invest.

Would you care for another example of persistent 'truths'? Just try to track down the evidence behind the statement that people can become immune to bedbug bites. Albrecht Hase in 1917 stated that he no longer responded to bedbug bites after being subject to about 2,500 of them. Neither Hase nor anyone else later reaffirmed this statement, yet the fact that 'some people' gain immunity against bedbug bites seems irremovable from textbooks.

6 Bug Dare

In previous chapters we have seen that the bedbug is evil, gruesome, stealthy and an agent of psychological stress. Does working with bedbugs, therefore, require an element of daring, if not heroism? Given the competition in the research world to be the first to uncover this or that detail of the bedbug's biology, this conclusion may not be too far from the truth: work with bedbugs, write about bedbugs and become a brave, courageous, cool and daring guy! Indeed, mostly guys – there are few female researchers working on bedbugs, and certainly few female pest controllers. One of the latter to prove the rule is Diana Kaufman in Ben Winters's *Bedbugs*, who is described with rather masculine attributes.[1]

It is certainly the case that bedbug research gets more press attention than much other insect research, which is no small advantage in the research world, where marketing your results has become part of the game. Research on bedbugs also is easily more memorable. Should a talk on bedbugs bore the audience, just show a picture of how bedbugs feed on human volunteers, or produce a picture of the bedbug penis and explain how it works, and the audience's attention is certain to come back. That's how I do it, anyway. If neither trick works, just feed them on yourself and you are a star, at least by YouTube's definition: an unremarkable video clip showing someone feeding a pot of bedbugs on his arm through a gauze net attracted 8 million views on YouTube within a few weeks. I wasn't aware that feeding bugs on yourself was linked to extrovert masculine behaviour until I looked again at one of our publications showing the effect of bites on humans. Look at the strong male arm with clenched fist on the next page, the man withstanding the bedbugs' vicious bites – no more needs to be said about heroism.

My late colleague Dr Camilla Ryne, who died in 2012, capitalized on the elevated reputation associated with feeding bugs. At Lund University in Sweden she investigated the chemical substances that bedbugs use to communicate with each other. As she herself showed quite a strong reaction to the bites, she needed volunteers to feed the bugs and paid them in a clever way: she had T-shirts produced proclaiming 'I fed the bugs'. What a trophy – and indeed she never ran out of volunteers.

Thousands of bedbugs are kept around the world with the purpose of testing susceptibility to various pesticides, to train dogs to the bedbugs' scent, to study their reproduction, to look at their genetic make-up or how they cope with the enormous stretching of their skin after feeding. Bedbugs need to be kept on blood and they only like warm blood, which must be provided through skin. The early researchers used mice, or rats, or themselves to feed

Illustration from a scientific article by Albrecht Hase, 1939. A mouse confined in the cage has its tail introduced into a small tube containing bedbugs and so serves as a blood source.

Fig. 4. Fütterung von Wanzen mit Hilfe einer Glastube. Nähere Erklärungen im Text.

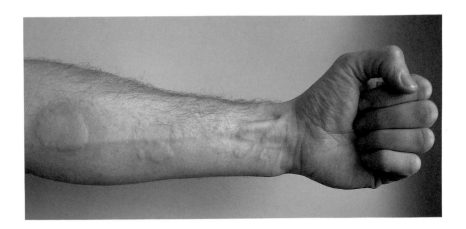

bedbugs. Usinger depicts some imaginative devices to strap a wooden frame for bedbug feeding onto guinea pigs or rats, even bats. Hase developed self-sustained cultures fed on mice, in which fatalities were not always prevented: in one case, a poor mouse had to put up with 180 bedbugs and did not live to tell the tale. Hence, using mice and rats poses a problem, because they themselves need to be kept happy and fed, including when researchers are away from the laboratory for a while. When Usinger acquired a set of new and rare bedbugs, he did not want to leave them in the lab in somebody else's hands, or on their arms, for that matter. Usinger employed an apparatus originally designed for lice to keep the valuable bugs with him, strapped around his body like a harness to be put on during his travels.

Feeding bedbugs on oneself has gone out of fashion because ethical guidelines do not look at it favourably (despite millions of people being bitten every day). The use of rabbits, chickens and mice has also decreased, probably for the simple reason that the administrative and veterinary supervision required for their safekeeping as food sources makes them prohibitively expensive.

Effects of bedbug bites on the skin, showing bites from 150, fifty and five bugs (left to right). Note the heroic posture: the strong masculine arm and clenched fist.

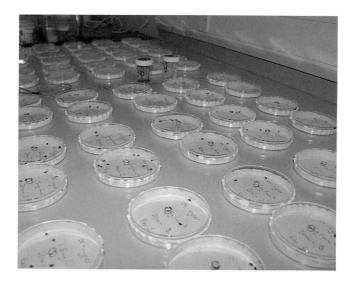

A solution is to trick bedbugs into feeding by offering them plastic membranes placed above warm blood. Some researchers have tried condoms as membranes. In my laboratory, however, the technique worked only moderately well and we abandoned it, partly due to the difficulty of justifying to our research funders why condoms might be needed in our bedbug research. Once the laborious business of feeding is solved, though, bedbugs are easy to keep, requiring little more than some moisture, room temperature and a feed every now and then.

Should a laboratory stock of bedbugs become depleted, or should other stocks or species of bedbugs become needed for comparison, there are many different ways to catch bedbugs. The hero of all bug catchers was again Robert Usinger. He was not only the most important and influential bedbug researcher of all time, he was also determined to catch any bug he wanted. For this he travelled worldwide and was incredibly imaginative, employing a long and unique list of methods to catch bugs: paying street boys in Mexico for every bug collected from their homes; wading through water tunnels to reach bat hosts; crawling through the Egyptian pyramids in scalding hot and dusty air; or cutting down trees in which fish-eating bats lived (to get those very specific fish-eating-bat bugs, *Latrocimex*). My favourite method involved blowing up the edge of a cliff with the help of the U.S. Naval Medical Research Unit (NAMRU). The species that Usinger discovered in the debris was new to science, and he named it *Stricticimex namru*. What a man! Compared with him how unimaginative and unadventurous were the methods used by other researchers, such as visiting well-known caves, putting double-sided sticky tape on cave walls, or sieving through material from henhouses or pigeon lofts. One of Albrecht Hase's methods, however, comes close in originality but is certainly unmatched in tastelessness. During the First World War Hase worked on

An unconventional way to feed bedbugs. The folded filter paper in each pot serves as a hiding place. The lid is covered with gauze to facilitate the blood feeding. Cultures can be handled with minimal effort.

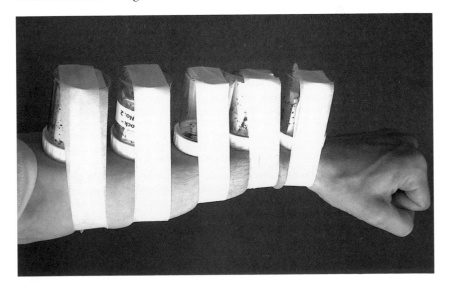

A device to feed bedbugs. Dried blood is dissolved and the solution injected between the membrane-covered compact discs. The compact discs are attached to an electrical device, which allows an easy warming of the blood to 37°C (98.6°F), to mimic normal human body temperature.

the Polish–Russian border, cutting the walls of wooden houses belonging to people who had fled the war zone. In this way Hase intended to show the hiding places of bedbugs in Russian houses (in this case in the cavities around the timber logs). He also experimented with the beds of people who had fled so recently that the beds still contained bugs. One of the striking practical recommendations from his research was that military personnel occupying houses in the war zone should move the beds away from the wall.

Usinger's autobiography, dictated from his sickbed just before his death, does not reveal a thirst for fame. This, of course, did not prevent him from becoming famous or others from striving to match his achievements. I certainly would not mind having a foot or two in one of his gigantic footprints, but my attempts to locate bedbug species look pathetic compared to Usinger's. Starting with normal bedbugs, my first encounter was in a seaside town in southern England where, luckily, the local communal pest controller was on holiday when an infestation was reported. This meant that my colleagues and I had two days to collect the bedbugs before his return. The bugs in the apartment where the infestation was reported had obviously been vacuumed away just before our arrival, but there were still bedbug skins everywhere, sticking to furniture, toys, beds and carpets. The most impressive discovery was in the low inner side of the chimney in the fireplace. What looked like white fur was in fact extremely tightly packed bedbug eggs, deposited in a regular arrangement, as neat and dense as blades of grass in an English lawn. While we were grateful for this unique experience, on our way home in the car we experienced for the first time in our lives that special bedbug shiver going down our spines. Nevertheless, we had collected a good stock of bedbugs and these were maintained in the lab for years.

Robert Leslie Usinger (1912–1968), the eminence of bedbug research.

My colleagues reported a grimmer experience in London, which resulted in the finest, best-thriving bedbug stock we have ever possessed (F4, for the record). An elderly man showing slight signs of self-neglect was sitting on the sofa in his flat when they arrived at the infestation site. The bedbug smell that greeted them promised a rich harvest, but they would not need the smell to identify them, since the bedbugs were active during the day, something that usually only happens in the safety of laboratory cultures. The most striking experience for my two colleagues, however, was not that the bugs were active on the man – they crawled

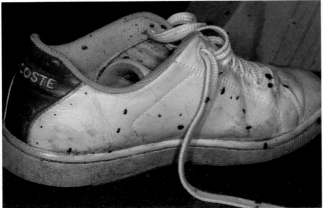

Bedbugs can accidentally be carried around with clothes, or be distributed with second-hand furniture or suitcases.

Most species of bedbugs live in bat caves. Sometimes bat caves harbour dangerous diseases and scientists studying bedbugs may be required to wear protective gear.

over him! – but that he brushed them off his clothes with his hand and announced that, while they collected the bedbugs, he would go down to the local pub for a pint. And he did.

KEEP THE MYTHS SIMMERING

In 1905 Alexandre Arsène Girault from Washington, DC, summarized the current scientific literature on the bedbug. He was 'very forcibly struck' by 'the great disproportion between the literature en masse, and the real facts now known concerning its habits and life-history. The great majority of the accounts are simply re-compilations and appear to have no other purpose than to cover so much space in as rapid a manner as possible.'[2] This same sentence could easily be written today. However, there may be reasons for the wealth of bedbug mistruths that go beyond merely filling the pages in publications. For example, if you are daring by nature, or a scientist in need of research funding, it might pay to keep talking about bedbug threats and infestations, how bedbugs might one day transmit diseases, and stress the importance of any

The earliest depiction of bedbugs. An infested bed, from Mattioli's *Di Pedacio Dioscoride Anazarbeo della materia medicinale* (1568).

research on this topic. If you are the cool type, however, you could produce a musical about bedbugs, or do as we do and take part in public talks with live bugs feeding on our arms – the ultimate display of bravado.

Over the years I have observed five strategies that stoke bedbug fearmongering. The first involves the presentation of usually abhorrent, or at least exaggerated, pictures of bedbugs. This strategy

Detail of Hase's educational wall poster: a heavy infestation in a 'wooden bed'.

Fig. 10 Teile eines Holzbettes mit Wanzenansiedlung
(Eier, Eischalen, Teile von leeren Larvenhäuten und Kot)

might have started with the first depiction of a heavily infested bed in a woodcut in a 1568 edition of Pietro Andrea Mattioli's *Discorsi*. Extreme infestation sightings can also be found on Hase's educational poster, in our own scientific articles and in many videos on the Internet – or as part of medical research, where extreme responses to bedbugs are shown regularly, whereas regular responses are shown rarely. This is understandable, because a bedbug bite on someone's neck is as unspectacular as any other small red spot. However, a dramatic picture with a row of unusual red bedbug bites along a cheek or an upper arm, ideally from a small child, ideally with its eyes wide open – that's quite something. One textbook showing the foot of an obviously neglected person implicitly suggests the unproven connection of bedbugs to poor hygiene.

The second strategy is the use of military language to characterize bedbug behaviour. 'Armies' of bedbugs that 'march' in 'marshalled formations' are presented by writers from Aristophanes to Flaubert, Orwell and Sheldon Lou. This language implies a cohesive and precisely governed bedbug entity, which generates the idea of an *enemy* or of a force to be reckoned with. Nadar and Bataille's *La Grande Symphonie héroïque des punaises* describes paratroops led by a 'general', who even mobilizes bugs to action, holds military parades and organizes reconnaissance missions. Military phrases are not conducive to peaceful thoughts.

The third strategy is the widespread use of comparisons out of all proportion to reality. Bedbugs have been described to be as big as a bed, or better still, as big as a house. Bedbugs are worse than sharks or lions, as the German playwright Bertolt Brecht claimed, or they were compared to a herd of elephants, as Heinrich Heine wrote a hundred years earlier. In China bedbugs were described as being more clever than the people equipped with Chairman Mao's thoughts, apparently the ultimate out-of-proportion metaphor in China.

Fourthly, bedbugs are frequently not mentioned alone, but with horrible company. It is often not just 'bedbugs', but 'rats, and mice and flies and frogs and bugs and lice', as Johann Wolfgang

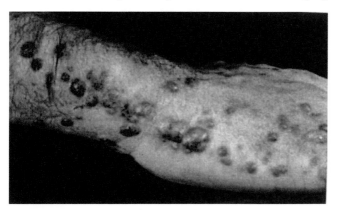

Exceptionally strong skin reaction in response to bedbug bites. Such responses are very rare and are overrepresented in the medical literature.

von Goethe had Mephistopheles say in *Faust*. On a contemporary porcelain plate, a bedbug is shown to meet with a flea (and even fares more evil than the flea!). The ever so heroic German biologist Ernst Haeckel placed them in verbal company with lice, fleas and cockroaches. Blood-sucking parasites, vermin and leeches were the company Lenin chose for bedbugs, while Himmler named them alongside lice, fleas, mosquitoes and horseflies when he ordered the foundation of an entire institute dedicated to their study.[3] During the Cultural Revolution in China, a campaign was run to eradicate 'sparrows, rats, flies and mosquitoes' as enemies of the people. The resulting mass killing of all birds and not just sparrows resulted in famine, and the enemy was quietly renamed as rats, bugs, flies and mosquitoes. In Chapter Eight we will see more consequences of unpleasant associations with bedbugs.

The final strategy to keep the myth simmering is to worsen the discomfort associated with bedbugs. Forecasts only see bedbug

Military language is often used to characterize the bedbug and to exaggerate its danger. This poster by the Spanish Association for Pest Control reads: 'The bedbug attacks from the trenches.'

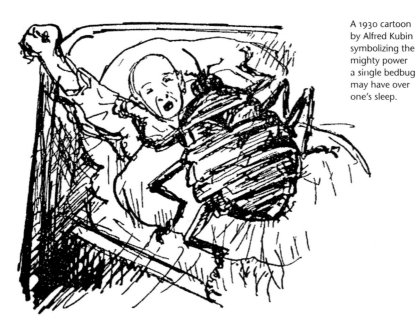

A 1930 cartoon by Alfred Kubin symbolizing the mighty power a single bedbug may have over one's sleep.

infestations increasing (sharing a characteristic with stock fund managers who only ever predict their shares' value to increase). Interestingly, bedbugs don't transmit diseases as many other blood-sucking insects do. In hundreds of experiments there has never been any proven transmission. Of course, bedbugs can take up the disease agent when sucking blood from an infected host, and it can thrive in the bedbug for some time. Yet the bedbug does not transmit the disease to a host. Despite this, it seems better to retain the bedbug as an enemy by stating in newspaper articles, books and on websites – just simply everywhere – that bedbugs have not *yet* been shown to transmit diseases. The loophole of fear is kept open, helping musical tickets sell, pest control companies flourish, bedbug books sell and research continue. I certainly play this card and see little chance of changing that.

A rare occurrence on a porcelain plate of a bedbug and a card-playing flea. Here, the bedbug is the evil card-sharper whereas the flea, the poor, exploited creature, calls for our sympathy. Illustration by A. Paul Weber, 1980.

Neglecting the history of scientific discoveries, a research project nowadays has to be proven to be relevant to the public more or less immediately. Non-immediate or merely foreseen potential benefits from research project proposals are not enough to secure research funding. This is why it might be wise to write on every application for a research grant involving bedbugs that they have not *yet* been shown to transmit diseases.

As in other historical cases, such eminent or exaggerated threats posed by bedbugs seem to leave only one possible option: declaring war.

7 Declaring War on Bugs

Control of bedbugs has tested man's ingenuity for centuries.
R. L. Usinger (1966)

The Spanish word for bedbug, *chinche*, has the interesting parallel that *chinchar* means 'to get on somebody's nerves'. Going beyond *chinchar* may resemble the psychological malady some sufferers, or supposed sufferers, of bedbug infestations experience: to bug out, or to go 'barmy as a bedbug' as in Roald Dahl's *The Twits*. Bedbugs, or the 'terror by night', as J.F.D. Shrewsbury, professor of bacteriology at Birmingham, called them in *The Plague of the Philistines*, needed to be controlled in order for one to have a peaceful night. This brought on some imaginative ideas.

The Spanish refer to many things dying in a short space of time as *morir como chinches*. One should assume, then, that at some historical point in the Spanish-speaking world there must have been a remedy to make bedbugs die very quickly. What was it? Was it related to the magic remedy that John Southall mentioned in his 1730 *A Treatise on Buggs*, a bug-destroying 'liquor' he had obtained in Jamaica? He claimed that in the instant he applied it, 'vast Numbers did come out of their holes, and die before my face.' And not only that, the substance was long-lasting and worked in the cold winter. Unfortunately the recipe for his long-lasting cure against bedbugs does not seem to have survived.

If bedbugs originated from bat-associated ancestors, what was early man's reaction to their cave-dwelling straw-mat fellows (the true wall-lice, so to speak)? Did early humans regard them as a

Bedbugs in a bat roost in Serbia photographed during the night when bats are foraging (left) and during the day when bats are present.

nuisance to be eradicated? And if so, how did they do it? If the lifestyle of bugs back then was similar to today's wild *Cimex lectularius* in bat roosts, one is tempted to speculate that bedbugs were not necessarily greeted with great enthusiasm. Caves in Kenya harboured tens or hundreds of thousands of *Afrocimex constrictus*. These individuals are known to sit in dense clusters on the wall. Would early man have used fire to burn as many of them as possible? Burning bugs remains popular into the present day. In 2015 a man was reported to have set his car on fire when using an open flame to rid the car of bedbugs. Earlier, in 1884, a caricature was published showing the Statue of Liberty with a torch, ready to burn bedbugs (see Chapter Two). Builders in Manchester during the 1920s were instructed to use a blowtorch to remove bedbugs from firewood taken from demolished houses.[1] Symbolic burnings of large models of bedbugs in 1930s England have been reported.[2] And of course, it has remained popular to burn infested fabrics and pieces of furniture.

Or was it perhaps better for our ancestors *not* to burn them? Were ancient bugs perhaps considered a sign of health, as fleas and lice allegedly were in ancient northern Europe? Or were they a divine signal, as the swarms of migratory locusts that invaded ancient China were believed to be? The locusts were supposedly sent by a deity to help the emperor and punish the bureaucrats. On a visit to Hopi land in 2012, I learned that bedbugs can be considered divine today. Their emergence in a house in spring was considered to herald the arrival of the Golden Eagles, which are the earthly connection to divinity.

Perhaps ancient man would have simply moved into different corners of the cave, or moved out for good in order to flee the pestering bedbugs. This behaviour is observed many times in today's humans. Numerous travellers have described having moved from the infested site (the bed) and slept on the table. Reverend James Woodforde (1740–1803) claimed he had 'sat up in a great Chair all night with my feet on the bed and slept very well . . . not pestered with Buggs'. George Kennan, whom we met earlier killing bedbugs in the Siberian town of Barnaul, claimed the same.[3] Henry, Lord Herbert, in Italy in 1750, 'used two tables and put a clean sheet over them' as a 'customary manner'.[4]

Or would ancient cave-dwellers have accepted bedbugs as something natural to get on with, as seen in today's Zambian proverb 'Where there are bats, there are bugs.' Over time, some

A dense aggregation of African bat bugs, *Afrocimex constrictus*, on the walls of a cave in Kenya.

knowledge of their habits may have accumulated and early man may have learned their lessons, similar to contemporary folk wisdom in Zambia passed on by a colleague: 'When I lift the mattress and see the bugs are engorged I will have a quiet night. If the bugs are flat, the night will be terrible.' This shows that knowledge of bedbugs and their inability to feed every night has long existed, even though there was no proper scientific proof until the 2000s.

Most of today's records suggest that bedbugs were not everybody's darling and that their numbers were controlled at an early stage of human history. This may have been additionally driven by the very welcome discovery of any new bedbug remedy, which served to heighten the discoverer's social status. Some examples exist today, but the self-promotion started as early as the foreword to John Southall's book, in which he sought to curry favour with the president of the Royal Society of London. However, these kinds of announcements also attracted early cynical notes. In 1823 a satirical statement in a German encyclopaedia mocked: 'Newton's and Kepler's great discoveries were not announced with as much pomp as nowadays is a new remedy for bedbugs.'[5]

About 2,500 years ago, Democritus suggested that hanging a hare's foot or a stag's hooves on the foot of the bed would help to defend against bedbugs. A few years later, a spell against bedbugs was written on a papyrus in ancient Egypt.[6] In the sixteenth century, Paracelsus in Basel recommended amulets of the sign of the scorpion to protect against bedbug infestations. Hoffmann reports a German regional custom involving standing naked in the room and addressing three walls with a certain spell.[7] Never mind the naked bit, strangely all of this had to happen on Good Friday, a time of year when temperatures in Germany would not usually have risen to a level causing bedbugs to crawl around and cause a nuisance. I am not aware of such practice in today's Germany, so the procedure may not have been very effective.

Another piece of practical advice against bugs concerned one of London's thousand lodging houses in 1850, namely to get 'half-drunk' in order to get to sleep.[8] In Germany Kurt Tucholsky satirized bedbugs, their eradication, their alleged thriving among the poor, and the German *Ordnung* all at the same time:

> Herewith it is to be added to the order concerning the extermination of pests in apartments with less than six rooms that shotguns against bugs are permitted only

Ronald Ginther, 'Fighting bedbugs and other vermin with fire. Although very dangerous, a tenant in slum dwelling in desperation uses kerosene to little avail', 1936. From the series *The Great Depression*.

between half past ten in the morning and a quarter to one. In the other hours of the day it is recommended to split the bugs with a table knife.[9]

One can safely conclude that bedbugs were not liked. People sought relief in designing their sleeping places, in applying their thumbs, applying heat, traps, plants, and later chemicals to kill bedbugs. Eventually this fuelled an entire industry, but the resulting relief will perhaps only ever be temporary.

PRESSING BUSINESS

Squashing a bedbug brings immediate death to the bedbug and satisfaction to the squasher. However, squashing a bedbug leaves a mark. In fiction, these marks, coupled with the secluded nature of bedbugs, are used to indicate the uncleanliness of a place. John Steinbeck's Danny in *Tortilla Flat* even catches bedbugs, squeezes them dead on the wall and draws faces around them, naming them after the mayor and particularly disliked members of the City Council. Surprisingly often, however, the spots resulting from squashed bedbugs are also described in positive ways. The spots look 'beautiful' or, by means of a few pencil strokes, are turned into a flower. Gustave Flaubert went the furthest with his praise of bedbugs. In bed with Kuchuk Hanem, a prostitute he met at Esneh on the Nile, and after an apparently satisfying sexual experience, Flaubert enjoyed squashing the bugs that walked along the wall. He described how they would form beautiful red and black arabesques, and, as he later wrote in defending the presence of bedbugs in the prostitute's bed, the smell of squashed bedbugs seemed to contribute to his sexual arousal. Admittedly, this episode is a digression from methods of controlling bedbugs, but it shows an acceptance of them or, in Flaubert's case, an appreciation that may perhaps make one pause before calling the pest controller. To digress a little further, we are not informed by Flaubert how frequently Kuchuk Hanem received guests, but the red and black arabesques are telling in that only the red ones can arise from recent blood meals. Black smears clearly must be from bedbugs enjoying Kuchuk Hanem or her visitors on previous nights.

Squashing blood-filled bugs is not liked by all, because it is often your own blood that you spill. Not surprisingly, alternative methods emerged. It is widely believed that the Berlin name *Tapetenflunder* (wallpaper flounder) relates to the flat bedbug as it is when starved. However, *Tapetenflundern* also form when you put a heated iron on it, in this case creating a particularly flat flounder. The hot iron offers a fine transition to the next topic, thermal warfare.

THERMAL WARFARE

In real caves, as well as artificial ones – otherwise known as flats or apartments – temperatures do not change as much as in the outside world over the course of the day or the year. We know this from temperature recordings in caves, apartments and, yes, in beds. Again, the bedbug was the causative agent when such measurements started in London in the 1930s. In Oakworth Road, Ladbroke Grove, temperatures in cold, unheated bedrooms were compared to fully heated living rooms and, based on these differences, it was calculated how many bedbugs would emerge and persist in each of the rooms.

Bedbugs don't like it too hot or too cold. High heat kills them instantaneously, just as heat kills almost any other living thing. Bedbugs, however, harbour little microbial guests called symbionts, which are killed at even relatively low temperatures: two

Cecil Johnston measured temperature variation in differently heated rooms in a house on Oakworth Road in London in the 1930s. He then used the temperature profile to predict bedbug infestation growth in such rooms. The same house photographed in spring 2010, inhabited by dwellers that might be unaware of the significance of their home for bedbug research.

weeks at 30°c seems sufficient. These symbionts provide the bedbugs with vitamin B and at high temperatures the supply of vitamin B dries up, bringing their reproductive activities and perhaps their lives to a halt. A way of ridding bedbugs worldwide is to place infested furniture or bedsteads in the heat outside. In 1932 a bedstead in the Darfur area of Sudan was 'left out in the noon-day sun. I thought, at first, that the undersides of the horizontal supports joining the legs were lined with snakeskin, but the pattern was formed of bed bugs, sheltering from the vertical rays, and overlapping like fishes' scales.'[10] Maasai people in the Mount Suswa area of Kenya told me in 2004 that it is still common to place a bed into the sun to reduce bedbug numbers. The illustrator and author Edward Ardizzone (1900–1979), when travelling with British troops to Egypt via Italy, observed the employment of extra heat to kill bedbugs on 1 October 1943 in Naples: 'Man with a blowpipe goes round my bed to kill bugs, a bad omen.'

A more modern version of this method that allows larger-scale treatment is the heat 'bomb' employed for persistent infestations: an entire apartment is heated to up to 70°c, so that there is no chance of survival for bedbugs. Heat is an elegant solution, because it seems evolution-proof: few organisms can survive temperatures above 90°c and bedbugs are not among them. If there are no survivors, there will be no resistant bugs either. However, the heat treatment of entire houses to eradicate bedbugs is not so modern. In 1918 a four-room house in Canada was cleared of every living thing after seven hours of sustained heating at 60–80°c. While effective and evolution-proof, heat treatment has a decisive disadvantage as it is expensive and not particularly furniture-friendly. As early as 1917 there were already efforts to replace it with cyanide.

Temperature also works at the opposite end of the scale. There have been several reports of soldiers placing their clothes outside on winter nights to freeze bugs, lice and everything else. Freezing your belongings is usually less effective than heat, however, and the normal household freezer may not be up to the job.

FIGHTING BY DESIGN

Placing a bed into the sun to rid it of bugs is dependent, of course, on the previous invention of beds. The luxury of having a dedicated household item on which to sleep has perhaps prevailed because it provides peace of mind to the sleeper: being off the ground gives a feeling of protection from animals crawling over the floor.[11] The peace may be short-lived, however, because a dedicated place often has the downside that its position in the room is fixed, providing a good opportunity for bugs to settle nearby and turn the place into their land of milk and honey. It is open to speculation in how many regions the hammock came into use, not so much because it is comfortable, but because it may reduce the number of visits made by crawling visitors.

John Southall asked for half a guinea for ridding the most elaborate bedsteads and six shillings for a plain four-poster. Clearly, elaborate beds meant more work for him. He also recommended keeping bed constructions simple, without much decorative woodwork, one of the first attempts to control bugs by bed design. What else is there on offer?

Shielding the bed legs. Lev Tolstoy described placing the legs of a bed into bowls containing water, petroleum, oil or paraffin. This method is recommended worldwide in dozens of old household advice books and magazines, and in official health documents. A somewhat related idea was noted in the Balkans in 1927 by a Herr von Bogdandy, who observed how people placed bean leaves on the floor around their beds. Bedbugs would crawl onto the leaves and sit paralysed in the leaves' dense layers of hair; the leaves could then be collected and the bugs destroyed. Von Bogdandy stated that bedbug eradication was complete using this method, and that he had removed up to 1 kilogram of bugs from a heavily infested room.[12] An adult bedbug weighs about one to two milligrams, and when bloated with blood it can weight up to ten. Herr von Bogdandy must therefore have collected somewhere between 100,000 and 1,000,000 bedbugs from one room using just bean leaves. Perhaps it was not quite 1 kilogram, or perhaps he weighed the bugs together with the leaves. No matter, the method itself was later repeated and the results were confirmed in the u.s.[13] By contrast, Albrecht Hase in Berlin failed to confirm the power of bean leaves to attract bedbugs, hold them fast and paralyse them. Fortunately this result was buried in the footnote of another publication.[14] If it had been known, no funding agency would have agreed to sponsor research in 2013 into the entrapment power of leaves, which showed that some of the hairs on leaves can indeed entrap live bedbugs.[15] The scientists even built artificial materials mimicking this hairy leaf surface that seemed to work against bedbugs. One is itching to see when, or if, this material might enter the future design of bed legs.

Bed nets. Ancient beds were never without a fine mesh against mosquitoes.[16] This was certainly effective against bedbugs too, and it seems that today it may be even more important to use bed nets in malarial areas against bedbugs than against the disease-carrying mosquitoes themselves.[17] Bed nets continue to be recommended for the mental peace of children afraid of creepy crawlies.[18]

Metal beds. The oldest known bed, 7,000 years old, is a four-legged stead with an under-mattress, a type allegedly still in use in modern-day Sudan.[19] Beds made of palm wicker were also used in Egypt for a long time, but thousands of those provided to British troops at the Suez Canal in 1914 had to be burned because they proved to be overly attractive to bedbugs. Perhaps it is not the beds alone that are to be blamed.

During his imprisonment, Fyodor Dostoyevsky cursed the wooden beds that 'because of some predisposition can never be free of bugs'.[20] The *nary*, one of three types of beds described in a German review on Russian pest control in the 1920s, consisted of wooden boards spanning the entire width of the room, which were embedded into the walls on either side. These were full of cracks and holes, being the 'perfect breeding sites for vermin, there celebrating triumphs in development, nutrition and repro-duction'.[21] The same type of bed was described by Alexandre Dumas on his travels through the Caucasus in 1858. In the case of the German review, however, the description fulfils another purpose. It was not only the wooden bedsteads, or planks, that harboured bedbugs. In an allegedly neutral, scientific analysis, it implies that the unclean, technologically deprived Russians must have bedbugs more often than the clean, hygienic and orderly Germans, who soon would be turning into *Herrenmenschen* (superior beings). However, contemporary German literature speaks a different language concerning the extent of infestations then current in Germany.[22]

One of the first attempts to reduce the presence of bedbugs in beds by changing the design of the bed was to use different materials: 'Young Lady Catherine Brydges, granddaughter of the great Duke of Chandos, after one bite, had her cradle lined with slips of bitter wood imported from Jamaica, and was never troubled again.'[23] That bedbugs preferred some types of wood over others had also been stated by John Southall, but little evidence has been provided, even to the present day. Then came the 'healthy brass beds' that replaced the 'majestic microbe traps' in early and mid-nineteenth-century England, in response to 'an Industrial Revolution to provide the masses with both tubular metal bedsteads and living conditions unhealthy enough to make them a necessity'.[24] In the nursery of Louis-Charles, son of Louis XVI and Marie Antoinette, everybody was said to have slept on metal bed frames, including the servants.[25] A few years earlier, in 1772, a French advertisement described such beds as bug-proof. Similarly, as Samuel Sharp observed in a letter from Florence in 1766, 'In the hospitals at London, bugs are frequently a greater evil to the patient, than the malady for which he seeks an hospital.' An item in the *St Thomas Hospital Gazette* of 5 August 1767 states that two wards voluntarily introduced metal beds, 'alleviating the terrible Inconvenience the Patients suffered from the Bugs', and another hoped for a hospital-wide introduction of metal beds.

These reports do not conclusively say that metal beds were introduced for the purpose of fighting bedbugs, but John Evelyn's diary contains a hint that this is what might have happened: 'for the most part the Bedsteds in Italy are all of forged Iron gilded, since tis impossible to keepe the wooden ones from the Chimices' (29 September 1645). While being the first such report, one would have to trust in the proper manufacture of these metal beds. In 1780 Lord Herbert, now 10th Earl of Pembroke, was informed on a visit to a hospital in Montpellier that metal beds are no 'obstacle to Buggs . . . if the Joints of the Bedstead are not kept perfectly clean'.[26] Beds forged of gilded iron had apparently been in use in old Pompeii. While their effectiveness is unknown, bedbugs were well known to have been around in Rome at the time before Pompeii drowned in ash and lava.[27]

Somehow, however, bedbugs seem to have managed to turn into metal-bed-bugs. In 1954 an authoritative account announces that the material of the bed 'whether wood or metal, doesn't make any difference and bugs can hide well in either'.[28] In Sheffield an elderly gentleman told me of his wartime experiences in Italy. When the troops arrived at an empty hospital, everybody was relieved to finally be able to sleep in a real bed. Within a short period of time, however, everyone climbed out of bed and found the hollow metal tubes simply teeming with bedbugs. The soldiers resorted to the usual methods by blowing them into the fire by the thousands, moving the beds near the heat of the fire, or sleeping on the floor.

Canopy. In 1883 the curator of the Berlin Museum of Natural History was plagued by bedbugs. Combining defence with research, he built a defensive device by placing large sheets of paper above his bed and pasting concentric circles of glue around them to prevent bedbugs that dropped from the ceiling from escaping. He then recorded the daily number of bugs caught, and claimed to have completely cleared the room of bedbugs.

Eighty years later the East German writer Erwin Strittmatter described a remarkably similar structure, this time covering the bed with parchment paper. The parchment had an interesting effect: bugs dropping onto it would make a noise that he described as 'penk' – a beautiful description, and perhaps the only existing acoustic representation of bedbugs. Perhaps the sound of bedbugs dropping onto parchment paper might have been slightly less somniferous than the sound of rain dropping on a windowsill.

Bedding. Bedbugs may have also shaped fashion trends in bedding. The introduction of cheap cotton ware in the nineteenth century was believed to be an important development in keeping bug numbers low. Cotton beddings could be washed at high temperatures without damaging the material, in contrast to the damask silk beddings that would not survive a hot wash – a disadvantage for the rich, for a change.[29] Two hundred years after the introduction of cotton bedding, scientists tested experimentally what temperature exactly would be needed to kill bugs in a hot wash. The scientists designed small packs of cotton, 'sealed with a sandwich bag clip', into which they placed 'ten adults, 10 third instar nymphs, and 10 eggs', and handed them into a laundry together with some clothes. To make sure the laundry did their job correctly, they also smuggled temperature recorders into the

A bedbug trap used through the centuries. The trap was placed under a pillow or mattress. The bugs crawled through the holes in order to seek shelter and stayed inside the tube. The next morning the tube was taken out and the bugs destroyed.

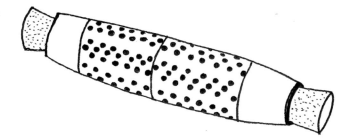

washing. Clearly, a thorough wash at 60°c, but not at 40°c, killed all the life stages of bedbugs.[30]

Bug traps. More directly targeted at individual bugs, between the seventeenth and nineteenth centuries bedbugs were caught, or at least baited, by traps in Sweden, India and Germany (and probably elsewhere). The trap was nothing more than a piece of hollow round timber with holes scattered around, and the ends were closed off with corks. It was placed in the bed or under the pillow at night. When the duvet was lifted in the morning the bugs were exposed to light and they ran away, seeking shelter in the small holes of the trap to feel snug. The trap was picked up, one of the corks removed and the bugs were blown into the fire or boiling water. This method was recommended in Indian hospitals as late as 1877 by a correspondent writing in the *British Medical Journal*. The bugs' search for darkness, for a rough surface and contact with other bedbugs (thigmotaxis, see Chapter Three), made this device quite effective. A number of bedbug traps currently sold are based on the same principle: a corrugated card box with a company label on it, nothing else. In France, placing corrugated paper under the bed was first recommended in 1916. These devices are not placed in the bed, but on the floor, and their effectiveness is far from universally accepted. Therefore, they must not be called traps, but 'interceptor' seems legally acceptable. Certainly, if a bedbug happens to reach an interceptor, the interceptor might intercept.

Another type of trap (sorry, interceptor) exploits the fact that bedbugs generally like to climb upwards. Placing containers that bedbugs can climb up into, but not out of again, near doors and around the legs of beds and tables is effective, and has had numerous uses, from modern interceptor companies to abundant references in historic and fictional literature.

There are also wicker traps, sometimes known as lobster-pots. These have 'flat sections of woven willow' to be tied under the bed. 'The French ambassador bought three' from the company G. W. Scott & Sons in London in 1782.[31]

Other design competitors had no more success than the interceptors. For example, the 1934 *Report on the Bedbug* published by the United Kingdom Ministry of Health recommended against the use of wallpaper, large skirting boards, wooden picture rails and wooden window boards. These recommendations were still upheld in 1966, but have, as is obvious in British houses, been neglected down to the present day – other more active forms of war against bedbugs were, and still are, required.[32]

CHEMICAL WARFARE

Historically, the first chemical deterrents of bedbugs were plants. Wild rosemary or marsh Labrador tea (*Rhododendron tomentosum*) was placed in babies' cots in Russia in order to keep bedbugs away.[33] This plant is called *klopovnik* in Russian, derived from *klop*, the word for bedbug. Intense use of this plant, which contains several insecticidal substances, has also been reported from Estonia and Sweden.

Other plants did not lend their toxins voluntarily to humans that sought alleviation from bugs. The plants either had to be burnt or be mixed with substances that would release their effective content. An early report about the chemical fight against bedbugs appears in the Chinese *Wei sheng yi jian fang* from 1423. In this report, detailed recipes are provided to burn the roots of a plant called *Stemona tuberosa* or to make a mixture of arsenic disulfide, tortoise carapace and buffalo horn. A mix of mule's hoof, buffalo horn, the Chinese quince and the Amur cork tree (*Phellodendron amurense*) could also be used. The tortoise shell was not tried, but all the other ingredients except cork were found to be effective when re-tested against bedbugs in 1940.[34] A recommendation from 1616, which involved burning a mixture of a species of the pepper family, aconite, arsenic sulphite and potassium nitrate, was also effective against bedbugs.

Fumigating houses and using other forms of chemical warfare against bedbugs flourished in England almost as early as bedbugs flourished. The most famous representatives of bedbug chemical warfare were, of course, John Southall, 'Maker of the Nonpareil Liquor for destroying Buggs and Nits', as well as Tiffin & Son, 'Bug Destroyers to Her Majesty and the Royal Family', which operated for more than 150 years from 1690. Later, the household recipes to drive away bedbugs became less secretive and actual experiments were done. The best-known recipes are those by the 'Chymist' Boyle Godfrey, who, just five years after Southall's *Treatise*, tried 'powdering most of the things found in the Druggist's-shop'. The results, published as *Miscellanea vere Utilia* (1735), are probably the first to prove the effectiveness of sulphur dioxide, or burning sulphur, 'which no Animal Life can subsist'. There was a timely second edition in 1737 and it is perhaps telling that this was reprinted in 2010. Godfrey gave exact instructions: 6 lb (2.7 kg) for rooms of 2,000 cubic feet or more, 4 lb (1.8 kg) for smaller ones, 'stopping the Chimney, by hanging blankets before it', and against the 'Cracks of the Door'. He even set safety standards: 'in the door a little Hole must be made, and cover'd afterwards with Glass, that may serve for a Peep-Hole to see no Mischief ensues.'

The components of the diverse recipes – all definitely effective – were so numerous, they are more a testimony to the existence of these substances in eighteenth- and nineteenth-century households than a proof of their effectiveness against bedbugs: garlic, resin, copper rust, ammonium salts, spirits, all kinds of insects, quicklime, bile, sulphur, vinegar, mercury (alone or mixed with egg white), soap, tobacco, and all kinds of combinations of these.[35] About 250 tinctures and powders were reported to have been on the market in Germany as insect-killing remedies.[36] In a kind of insect-level homeopathic approach, a women's magazine in 1898 recommended putting cockchafers in a jar filled with brandy to allow them to infuse, before using the liquid to paint the places inhabited by bedbugs.[37] Its impact on bedbugs is not documented, but it was certainly effective against cockchafers.

One of the most frequently mentioned remedies is petroleum, which contains sulphur. Upon burning it releases sulphur dioxide, a known potent killing agent. Sulphur is probably the effective component when current-day Hopi burn chilli on cedar wood to fumigate houses against bedbugs. When sulphur became available in pharmacies it partly replaced petroleum, possibly because it was more effective during burning. Petroleum had the advantage, however, that it could be painted onto bedsteads and into cracks in the walls. Sulphur's effectiveness against bedbugs meant that it became a favourite means of control in fictional literature, described by George Orwell, Sheldon Lou, Ruth Park and others, and as late as the mid-1980s by Clive Sinclair.

While sulphur dioxide turned out to be effective against bedbugs, it also bleached furniture, curtains, clothes and most things made of metal, so other solutions were more than welcome. Hydrocyanic acid (prussic acid) has been used for controlling all kinds of insects and other animals since the late nineteenth century. The story begins in 1877 with the discovery of *Ephestia kuehniella*, a small but voracious moth species whose larvae were causing huge economic damage in mills and flour stores. Already more than a nuisance at this time, its actions became life-threatening during the First World War, resulting in a desperate need to control the pest. Concurrently there was a serious problem with lice, which

Fritz Haber (1868–1934). German patriot, Jew and 'father' of the German poisonous gas war of the First World War. In Haber's laboratories, Zyklon B was invented.

The building today that harboured the laboratory of Fritz Haber in Berlin-Dahlem in the 1920s and 1930s, It was probably in this building that Albrecht Hase and Ferdinand Flury developed the chemical Zyklon, later to be Zyklon B. Hase and Flury tested Zyklon on three insect species, among them the bedbug in 1922.

also became an increasingly pertinent issue. To tackle it, the entomologist Albrecht Hase, who had recently joined Fritz Haber in Berlin, opened a laboratory in a prisoner-of-war camp in Russia in March 1915. There he carried out fundamental studies on the biology of lice and bedbugs that resulted in biological compendia that even today can be considered landmarks. Fritz Haber was the director of the Kaiser-Wilhelm Institute for Physical Chemistry and Electrochemistry. The association of bedbugs and lice to these two topics stemmed from Hase's experimentation with hydro-cyanic acid and his recognition of the potential of using this and similar gases to kill both warm-blooded creatures and insects.

As a result, in February 1917 Haber suggested founding a separate Kaiser-Wilhelm Institute for poison gas research. Its purpose was to continue experiments with toxic gases for military use, but also to promote studies with civilian applications, such as pest control. Even though this Kaiser-Wilhelm Institute of Applied Physical and Biological Chemistry, as it was to be called, was never established, Haber successfully lobbied (as we would say today) for a similar institute. He created enough momentum among the military, the civilian authorities, the chemical industries and scientists from various institutes to gain support to build a centralized authority responsible for the 'extermination' of lice and bugs. It is no surprise that the director of Degussa, a company that used enormous amounts of hydrocyanic acid for the production of gold, welcomed this development. With all this power in Haber's hands, it was in April 1917 that Albrecht Hase oversaw the introduction of large-scale hydrocyanic acid gassing as an effective new means of delousing the German army. Following this success, more industrial than scientific, the gassing technology was redirected to deal with the damaging moths that still lived in the flour mills. By August 1918 nearly 150 mills had been gassed, along with military facilities such as barracks, hospitals and delousing centres. This figure rose to 21 million cubic metres of gassed buildings by 1922.[38]

This technological success enabled Haber to incorporate poison gas research into the programme of his institute, even though this would have required delicate political negotiations, because the Treaty of Versailles did not allow Germany to carry out any research even remotely benefiting the military. Haber overcame this difficulty by founding a pharmacology department that enjoyed substantial secret military funding. It is very likely that parts of his gas research still served military purposes, as did the the neighbouring state-run, and closely connected, Biologische Reichsanstalt.[39] The head of the pharmacology department became – guess who – the louse and bug expert Albrecht Hase. In a series of experiments, he and his colleague Ferdinand Flury worked to synthesize certain chemical compounds with hydrocyanic acid. One of these compounds was a carbonic acid. In 1922 the two researchers published an article showing that this specific derivate of hydrocyanic acid was completely effective against (that is, it would completely eradicate) bedbugs, flour moths and cockroaches. This derivate was called Zyklon, the predecessor of Zyklon B.[40]

Zyklon B was used in several countries. It was a crystallized substance that was relatively safe for the handler, because the deadly gas would only be released upon contact with air, that is, when the tin was opened. To alarm the handler of a possible toxic release, a strongly smelling substance was added to Zyklon, but the ss soon ordered this component to be removed.

Most of the synthesized Zyklon B was used for pest control, and 400 tonnes were produced in Germany per year during wartime. Only 4 kg of Zyklon B, however, was enough to kill 1,000 people, and the 5 per cent of its annual production that was used to kill people was sufficient to cause the greatest tragedy in human history. The producers of Zyklon B, the infamous I. G. Farben and the Degussa enterprises, still exist today. Neither company was expropriated after the war, an unusual status that was otherwise only granted to the big German banks. Zyklon B remained in production in Dessau in East Germany until 1969. In West Germany it was sold as Cyanosil, and abroad it continued to be called Zyklon. Zyklon B is apparently still being produced under the trade name Uragan D2 at a factory in Kolin in the Czech Republic.

The historian Margit Szöllosi-Janze thinks that Haber's close connection to the military made him 'in no way reluctant to have his research work applied for military purposes, and clearly he pursued that application deliberately and in total awareness of the consequences . . . The other, and even more horrific, possible application of the research on poison gases, however, was absolutely beyond his imagination.'[41] In 1933 Haber left Germany and worked briefly in Cambridge. He died in Basel in January 1934, while on his way to a new position in Palestine. He thus escaped the ultimate gruesome irony of history – death by Zyklon B gas in a concentration camp. Many of Haber's family were not so lucky.

Around 1872 Othmar Zeidler at the University of Strasbourg brought together chlorobenzene, chloral and sulphuric acid in a chemical procedure known as the Baeyer condensation. As a result, he was the first to synthesize 2,2-bis-(p-chlorophenyl)-1,1,1-trichloroethane. Although this synthesis made no great impression at the time, Zeidler had discovered the substance we know today as the insecticide DDT. Robert Metcalf has pondered how the course of the Franco-Prussian War, the First World War and many other events might have changed 'had a stray insect crawled upon Zeidler's pile of shining crystals and the chemist had gained an inkling of the enormous powers of the insecticide'.[42] Instead the compound's potential remained hidden within the pages of an 1874 academic journal until Paul Müller in Basel stumbled across the article when systematically searching the scientific literature for all chemical compounds with a specific structure that he knew has insecticidal properties. It was patented in 1940 and Müller was awarded the 1948 Nobel Prize in medicine after the worldwide success of this potent insect killer, which could be dissolved and sprayed, remaining on surfaces for some time. It was also then considered to be harmless to vertebrates.

DDT was widely used from the early 1940s, but doubts were raised after reports in 1947 that DDT was no longer able to kill bedbugs in the Pearl Harbor barracks, where they had evolved resistance to the insecticide. At least another hundred insect species had, or would later, become resistant. By the 1960s DDT could no longer be used against bedbugs in many countries, including those in the Mediterranean and Korea. Britain was lucky to escape the evolution of DDT resistance for quite some time, and in 1964 Shrewsbury could still write that bedbugs 'can now be readily controlled' with it. The residual effect of DDT, however, was not only found on surfaces, but also within biological materials, causing serious damage in vertebrates. The problem was widely publicized in Rachel Carson's *Silent Spring* (1962), leading to a long campaign to ban DDT worldwide.

It is commonly stated that DDT contributed to the decline of bedbugs in the West, but the very little data on this shows this to be untrue. In the UK bedbugs declined dramatically from the 1930s, well before the use of DDT in the 1940s, and to a much greater degree than after its application. DDT contributed greatly to reducing malaria, but changes in the UK's housing schemes seemed much more instrumental in the decline of bedbugs.[43] This careful research, however, may have little effect: people continue to praise DDT's success in eradicating bedbugs, whatever their reason for keeping this myth alive.

BIOLOGICAL CONTROL

'Eco' is fashionable, so why not look into eco-friendly bedbug clearances? Here are a few suggestions, all historically proven, of course. My first recommendation is elegantly described in an awful nationalistic German novel set in 1930s Siberia.[44] If any part of that book is bearable, it would be the description of placing mattresses in the garden for chickens to freely pick the bedbugs off them. When coupled with the current boom in urban gardening, this generates a beautifully Dadaistic image of gigantic numbers of chickens on the roof gardens of New York, London and Berlin, picking bugs off mattresses placed up there for bedbug control.

My second suggestion is more serious and based on actual research. Few animals feed on bedbugs, apart from some spiders, ants and assassin bugs. Tolerate large numbers of these creepy crawlies and enjoy a lower load of bedbugs. It is perhaps not surprising that researchers have been reluctant to try this method on themselves, as they have done with so many others, but instead first used a refugee camp. The spider *Thanatus flavidus* is said to have reduced a strong bedbug infestation near Athens within two years: individual spiders are alleged to have consumed thirty to forty bugs per day, especially those that were fully engorged with blood. Albrecht Hase confirmed this spider's usefulness inside a hospital where small mammals were housed for experimentation, exterminating a large bedbug infestation within a year. A Second World War report states that soldiers were ordered to collect spiders and release them in their barracks, which for a few days resembled a web-clad fairy grotto. Afterwards, however, the bedbugs were allegedly gone. Only the realist Heinrich Kemper strongly disapproved of the idea that spiders could be effective in treating a global bedbug plague.[45] The only other biological methods I can offer are perhaps bean leaves or spraying fungal spores, neither of which make the home particularly cosy.

An alternative solution is the friendly – to some, anyway – and somewhat eco use of sniffer dogs. The downside is that these only detect the bugs but do not eat them. In 2006 the journal *Hotel and Motel Management* reported on the first specially trained bedbug sniffer dog, who could 'crawl into tight spaces that human inspectors cannot' in New York hotels and so paved the way for early bedbug detection and lower numbers of lawsuits.[46] She was alleged to be able to discover bedbugs even behind walls (perhaps something like the walls, thin as paper, described by George Orwell in Paris). An important advantage of sniffer dogs is that the pest control company might use a dog to prove that the room is bug-free after treatment. This proof of absence – a potent deterrent against claims that infestations are recurrent, rather than caused by newly introduced bedbugs – may be the recipe for these sniffer dogs' success in several countries, although I know of no independent study showing their success rate in detecting bugs.

It was mentioned earlier that bedbug colonies in the laboratory have a different smell. Interestingly, it seems that some bedbug colonies of *Cimex lectularius* are also able to escape the attention of sniffer dogs, which opens up the possibility that somewhere bedbugs can thrive undetected and are overlooked (or, rather, oversniffed) by dogs. Just as with resistance to DDT, and to the more recently developed pesticides carbamates and pyrethroids, which usually evolves within two to six years after their introduction, I wonder how long it will be before the first bugs appear that cannot be sniffed out any more – my bet would be as soon as the end of 2018. But perhaps this is not a problem and dogs just have to be retrained. Sniffer dogs to detect bedbugs are becoming big business, so we can probably expect some interesting developments. In fact, there are many animals that are much easier and quicker to train than dogs. Bees, for example, would probably take two days to train, with subsequently much easier maintenance.

It is apparent that no single remedy exists to control bedbugs, that human behaviour helps the bedbugs to survive and that bedbug management in large cities requires, as it always has, serious organizational efforts. It seems we will never get rid of bedbugs entirely. While most people may be aware of this, the continued presence of bedbugs also means that calls to eradicate them are regularly upheld. This has dramatic consequences when bedbugs are representatives of the unwanted Other.

DIE WANZE ALS KAMMERJÄGER

„Ich werde mein Haus doch noch von Ungeziefer rein kriegen!"

(33 Deutschen, darunter Heinrich Mann, Prof. E. J. Gumbel, Willy Münzenberg, Wilhelm Pieck, Ernst Toller, Kurt Tucholski, Lion Feuchtwanger, wurde die Staatsangehörigkeit aberkannt.)

8 The Other Bug

Centuries after it crawled into the English language, *bug* has become a household term for anything that doesn't work or causes some interruption to the life one is used to, as exemplified by the computer bug or stomach bug. Why is that? Why is it a 'bug'?

Things that do not function in the way we want them to are irritating. They cause trouble and extra work, and drive us outside our comfortable routines at unexpected and unwanted times. We often can't detect the bug in the first instance until we bring it to a specialist. The factor causing these problems is secretive, unfamiliar and causes painful interruptions to our lives that we are not prepared for – just like bedbugs. Perhaps it is not surprising that they – bedbugs – have lent their name to troublemakers.

EXTENDING THE BLAME, EXTENDING THE WAR

While disturbing our comfort, bedbugs also comfort our disturbance: they come from outside our world. Always. They are not part of our world. Never. They are strangers, aliens, foreigners and so on. Just like computer bugs, they are never our fault. If bugs are in one's house, they must have come from the neighbour, as we read in Karl von Frisch's *Twelve Little Housemates*, Ruth Park's

John Heartfield (originally Helmut Herzfeld) was a German communist who with his photocollages protested against the removal of civil liberties in Nazi Germany in 1933. Here he features a bedbug as a pest controller when the German Minister for Internal Affairs withdrew German citizenship from German intellectuals, such as Albert Einstein, Lion Feuchtwanger, Heinrich Mann and Kurt Tucholsky.

Harp in the South and George Orwell's *Down and Out in Paris and London*. This is known almost everywhere, and is confirmed in the ancient and modern scientific textbooks. One of the few exceptions is Sheldon Lou's narrative of shared dormitories in 1960s China. I wonder whether it is worth comparing Western and Eastern attitudes to bedbug infestations.

Eventually bugs have to come in from the outside. Their outside-ness makes bedbugs an excellent vessel to be loaded with all the characteristics that we do not want or want to get rid of. It does not seem to matter that almost every object in the world came from the outside at some stage in its life: bedbugs are *particularly* from the outside.

And not just from outside the house: bedbugs also always come from a neighbouring country. This is a trait they share with other unwanted subjects, like the German cockroach, the French pox or the Nanking bug. That every country in the world claims that bedbugs come from a neighbouring country may present good evidence for the bedbugs' divine origin.

By ascribing bedbugs an otherworldly status by portraying bedbugs as 'absolutely, totally not like us', and as being gruesome, disgusting, perfidious and evil, we are automatically separating ourselves from the bedbugs and saying that we, the non-bedbugs, are lovely, clean, fair and charming. By defining the Other we, in fact, define ourselves – a perfect societal function of the bedbug, and with cruel consequences.

Bedbugs smell strongly in a way that we happen to dislike, and in a way with which many of us are unfamiliar. Bedbugs can live among us unnoticed, but they may appear suddenly and become so commonplace that they can no longer be ignored in our private lives. Because we have not previously dealt with bedbugs, we really do not understand what is going on with them and why they suddenly appear. Bedbugs like to live in groups (because of their thigmotaxis) and gang together because it is useful to be in groups when the environment is unfamiliar. And perhaps the ganging seems hostile because to us – who know the environment – there is no need to hang around in groups.

One cannot help noticing that these bedbug- and vermin-associated characteristics provide an excellent metaphor for the unwanted, including unwanted groups of people. To understand this, read the preceding paragraph again, inserting the name of a group of people that you happen to dislike for every mention of 'bedbugs'.

The metaphorical comparison with bedbugs provides gruesome examples of the alienation of groups of people. The angst of the Other may be particularly effectively stoked by creating a common enemy. In reality, a common sense, a joint feeling can be achieved by controlling bedbugs: Dolour's quarrelling family in Park's *The Harp in the South* is suddenly united in declaring war on bedbugs. Bedbugs can be used metaphorically to maintain political power by externalizing problems and blaming the alienated group for those that already exist. The fact that dramatic language can change people's behaviour, and that hate speeches may finally ignite the flames of hatred, is something we have known since the experiences of Victor Klemperer (in whose home city of Dresden, and now mine, I can regularly hear hate speeches against strangers while I write this chapter). The result of such divisive language is the unbearable reality of dozens of millions of the dead, killed in acts of genocide after hatred had been incited by attributing to others terms such as blood-sucking, vermin, bugs, lice, cockroaches or pests, diminishing them and lowering the threshold at which it is permissible to kill or even eradicate them. Elihu Richter and Yael Stein have followed this bloody path through history and come to a simple conclusion: words kill.[1]

THE JEWISH OTHER IN THE THIRD REICH: ANTI-SEMITISM

A particularly intense period of anti-Semitism started in Germany in the early twentieth century, culminating in the systematic killing of millions of Jewish people during the Third Reich. One way to prepare the German people for the Holocaust was to employ specific language to describe Jewish people as blood-sucking pests, bedbugs and lice followed shortly by calls for their killing, eradication, extermination and mass murder. This was preceded by a linguistic shift from references to specific species that cause damage to particular crops towards using the generic word *Schädling* (pest), literally meaning damaging agent. Suddenly there was a word for anything damaging: the phrases 'extermination' and 'mass murder', first applied to 'pest' and 'vermin' in agriculture and forestry, underwent a similar development in society to now mean the treatment of social pests and parasites.[2] In Nazi Germany this meant those of Jewish birth. Terms were adopted to cover the development of social hygiene methods to clean the German *Volkskörper* ('nation's body'). The introduction of negative, biologistic language into society by those in power helped to pave the way for ordinary Germans to accept and support the Holocaust, and to make the Third Reich *judenrein* (clear of Jews). *Rein*, a word that could simply mean 'clean' or 'tidy', took on further meanings through its association with parasites: eradication, extinction, extermination, mass murder, mass execution and annihilation. Originally reserved for pest insects, and bedbugs in particular, these words were now augmented by similar phrases of contagion and connected with anti-Semitism, such as pestilence, plague and lice (the last only after it became known that lice were vectors for typhus). These words were meant to indicate that the Jewish, Sinti and Roma people not only sucked the blood from healthy Aryan *Volk*, but spread

132

diseases. One needed to keep away from these people or, better still, destroy them.

These anti-humane terms obviously used publicly in speeches by Hitler, Himmler and others also spread widely and entered common usage. Evidence of likening bugs and blood-sucking insects to Jewish people can be found almost everywhere: in letters written by soldiers from the front, in household magazines, in statements from the medical profession and the clergy, and in children's books. This makes for unpleasant reading and I will restrict myself to a few examples.

In the children's book *Der Pudelmopsdackelpinscher* (The Poodle-Pug-Dachshund-Pinscher, 1940), the Jews are likened to cuckoos (stealing other people's homes), hyenas (feeding on the sick and wounded), the chameleon (a deceiver), the venomous snake, the bedbug (blood sucker) and finally a fictitious dog made up of many breeds. This mongrel breed represented the debased and cross-bred genetic impurity of the Jews that needed to be exterminated. Indoctrination at an early age was very effective and lasted far beyond wartime, right down to modern times. As late as 1972 rebellious students were likened to *Wanzen* (bugs) by former Nazis such as the right-wing politician Emil Franzel, who called for their eradication. The continuing persistence of racist, and particularly anti-Semitic, opinions among older Germans was recently revealed throughout the population.[3] A statement in the *Zeitschrift des Deutschen Ärztebundes* (Union of German Physicians) in 1938 claimed:

> Rats, bedbugs, and fleas also appear in nature as do the Jews and Gypsies . . . We all have to wipe out these vermin and, therefore, today, change the essentials of their life, implement detention and sterilization measures so that the enemies of the Volk will be eliminated, slowly but surely.[4]

Karl Fiehler, a high-ranking ss officer from Munich, stated in 1937 that he did not deny that God had created Jews, but he likewise did not deny that God created bedbugs, lice and fleas. God, however, had not determined that humans were to be eaten by vermin – perhaps God created vermin in order for humans to get used to cleanliness. Fiehler's words clearly present the Jews as the unclean Other, thereby heightening his own status by suggesting that he is clean.

Anti-Semitism goes back much further than Nazism. Newspapers and magazines existed that were solely dedicated to anti-Semitism, such as *Der Eiserne Besen* (The Iron Brush). The metaphor of the blood-sucking, life-draining Jew was apparently created in the early nineteenth century. There were also religious predecessors. In 1896 the anti-Semitic Viennese priest and writer Sebastian Brunner stated that society would lose its Christianity and become governed by Jewry. In one of his satires, *Wanzen-Epos* (Bug Epic), he openly called Jewish people bugs, vermin and parasites, which could only be countered by 'Wanzenpulver' (anti-bug powder).[5]

Norman Naimark, summarizing the work of many others, provides this nightmarish picture promoted under the Third Reich: 'Jews also directly threatened the survival of German men and women. They seduced and impregnated innocent German girls, thereby weakening the Aryan blood of the nation . . . Inherently immoral, Jewish men gravitated towards pimping, pornography, and other forms of sexual deviance, spreading syphilis.'[6] Given that Jewish men were often accused of raping Aryan girls, it was perhaps fortunate that the male bedbug's behaviour during traumatic insemination was not widely known. Undoubtedly this would have been exploited in unimaginable ways.

Other disturbing views have been collated by Joanna Tokarska-Bakir. She shows that the belief that Jewish rabbis sucked blood

Ephraim Moses Lilien. An ironic illustration mocking the allegation of Jews drinking the blood of a Christian child. Derogative references to blood-sucking and parastic lifestyles have a long history in anti-Semitism. c. 1910.

out of Christian babies was widely held. This blood-sucking metaphor allowed the description of the Jews' 'parasitic habit' to expand into three areas: religious scaremongering of the Jews, as described above; Jewish-induced nationalistic fears, for which terms such as 'lice', 'locust' and 'plague' were added to the anti-Semitic repertoire after the Second World War; and the view of Jews as capitalists and bankers. Tokarska-Bakir also points out how the assignment of these cruel metaphors to generate the Other allowed a dichotomous language that benefited the ascriber, such as, bloodsucker/victim, theft/loss, criminality/innocence, strangeness/familiarity, brutality/humanity, aggression/martyrdom.[7]

The only light in the midst of this darkness of using bedbugs as a propaganda instrument was John Heartfield's humorous photomontage of the wolf in sheep's clothing that appeared on the front page of the *Arbeiter Illustrierte Zeitung* on 7 September 1933, months after both Heartfield and the magazine had been forced into exile in Prague.

One can only hope that pest and vermin metaphors will not be used again to invite thoughts of social segregation and eradication. Yet the simple-minded comparisons that address the lowest of human instincts show no signs of becoming extinct. The widely publicized Hutu radio propaganda that likened the Tutsi people to cockroaches resulted in 800,000 Tutsi deaths in Rwanda. It is to be hoped that most people's psychological over-reaction to bedbugs will not be exploited in a future genocide. The use of this very word 'genocide' against bedbugs, in connection with the word 'annihilation' in a catchy ballad in the musical *Bedbugs!!!*, was deeply disturbing.

THE RICH OTHER: ANTI-CAPITALISM

Less known, but perhaps as furious and barbarically effective as Nazi anti-Semitism, was Lenin's propaganda in the 'fight for life and death', which was the cleansing and eradication of the capitalists and the bourgeois in Russia. Lenin's suggestions of what to do with these so-called human vermin, parasites, fleas, villains and bugs were both shockingly precise and shockingly diverse. This policy was surpassed by Stalin, who widened the definition of vermin to anybody who did not comply with his views. It was at this time that *The Bedbug*, a play by the poet and former Soviet propagandist Vladimir Mayakovsky, was first performed in February 1929 at the Meyerhold Theatre in Moscow, with music by Dmitri Shostakovich. It is a satirical fantasy arguing that two ways of cleansing are required in society: first, the taste of the proletarian masses must be washed clean of any remaining bourgeois filth, and second, the Soviet cultural authorities needed to be cleaned from the bourgeois that suddenly presented themselves as loyal proletarians.

Poster advertising the premiere of Vladimir Mayakovsky's piece *Klop* (The Bedbug), in the Meyerhold Theatre, Moscow, on 12 February 1929.

Prisypkin (the word resembling scabies in Russian) is a middle-class man who leaves his proletarian girlfriend for a bourgeois one. As he prepares for the wedding in wintery Moscow, a bedbug

ГОСТЕАТР имени ВС. МЕЙЕРХОЛЬДА

КЛОП

Феерическая комедия
ВЛ. МАЯКОВСКОГО
5 действий (9 картин)

ПРЕМЬЕРА

1. ПОМАТРОСИЛ И БРОСИЛ...
2. НЕ ШЕВЕЛИТЕ НИЖНИМ БЮСТОМ...
3. С'ЕЗЖАЛИСЬ ИЗ ЗАГСУ ТРАМВАИ...
4. С ВИЛКОЙ В ГОЛОВЕ...
5. ВОДКОЙПИТАЮЩЕЕСЯ МЛЕКОПИТАЮЩЕЕ...
6. ДВИЖЕНИЯ НОРМАЛЬНЫЕ—ЧЕШЕТСЯ...
7. ЛОВЛЯ КЛОПА.
8. ТОЛЬКО НЕ ДЫШИТЕ!...
9. ПОРАЗИТЕЛЬНЫЙ ПАРАЗИТ...

ПРЕМЬЕРА

Год 1929
Год 1979

Постановка Народного Арт. Республики
ВС. МЕЙЕРХОЛЬДА

Музыка Д. ШОСТАКОВИЧА.
Танцы — Наталии ГЛАН.
Полет пост. Виталий ЛАЗАРЕНКО.
Трио гармонистов ГОСТИМ'а:
КУЗНЕЦОВ,
МАКАРОВ,
ПОПКОВ.

Оркестр ГОСТИМ'а
под упр. Ю. С. НИКОЛЬСКОГО.
У рояля — А. Г. ПАППЕ.

АКТЕРЫ (по алфавиту):

Атьясова, Башнатов, Бенгис, Блажевич, Боголюбов,
Бочарников, Генкина, Говоркова, Ермолаева, Зайчи-
ков, Злобин, Зотов, Игорь Ильинский, Нельберг,
Кириллов, Коган, Козиков, Норшунов, Костомолоц-
кий, Ладыгин, Лесс, Логинова, Логинов, Макарев-
ская, Мальцева, Маслацов, Мологин, Неустроев, По-
плавский, Савельев, Свердлин, Серебрянникова, Си-
бирях, Соколова, Старновская, Субботкина, Суворо-
ва, Суханова, Тамерин, Фадеев, Херасхова, Чикул,
Шмидт.

В спектакле занят весь состав студентов Госу-
дарственных Экспериментальных Театральных мастерских им. Вс. МЕЙЕРХОЛЬДА.

Ассистент (работа над текстом) Вл. МАЯКОВСКИЙ.

Режиссеры-лаборанты:
ЗИНАИДА РАЙХ, А. ЛОКШИНА.
А. НЕСТЕРОВ, П. ЦЕТНЕРОВИЧ.

Конструктор 1-й части (1, 2, 3, 4 карт.) —
Вс. МЕЙЕРХОЛЬД.

Цвет, костюмы, грим и вещество оформл. (1, 2, 3
и 4 карт.) сработ. художниками КУКРЫНИКСАМИ.

Художник-конструктор 2-й части (5, 6, 7, 8, 9 карт.)
костюмы, вещества, оформления—А. М. РОДЧЕНКО.

Макеты строил студент режфакультета
ГЭКТЕМАС'а — С. КОЗИКОВ.

Конструкции построены в собственных мастерских
под рук. А. ЧААДАЕВА и А. БЕННЕР.

Костюмы изготовлены костюмер. мастерской № 23
Рабис под набл. Р. БЕЛОЦЕРКОВСКОЙ.

Парики — В. Н. ШИШМАНОВА и Н. И. ИВАНОВА.

Директор театра
Народный Артист Республики
Зав. Адм.-Фин. частью Б. ГОЛЬДБЕРГ.
Зав. Хозяйственной частью Х. Л. МИЛЬНЕР.

ВС. МЕЙЕРХОЛЬД

gets into Prisypkin's clothes and settles in. When the wedding party gets out of control, the house catches fire. The fire brigade arrives to put it out, but the water freezes on the spot, trapping Prisypkin and his bug in the ice. Fifty years later, in 1979, they are brought back to life and find that in that time Soviet society has been carefully cleansed and a form of utopia created. As outsiders who represent the decadent old ways, Prisypkin and the bedbug are placed in a zoo. Instead of finding Prisypkin and his desires repellent to their utopian beliefs, however, the people are captivated by the joy he displays in dancing, lust and drinking beer. Mayakovsky's appeal to generating understanding, even empathy, for Prisypkin and his bug's bourgeois desires must have been a pinch of satire too far, even for him. Despite the play's popular success, Mayakovsky fell out of favour with Stalin, which some suggest contributed to his suicide on 14 April 1930.[8]

Just as in the Soviet Union at the time, the image of blood-sucking bankers and middle-class people parasitizing the working masses has remained a well-used phrase in many countries to the present day.

THE POOR OTHER

Bedbugs have no respect for class. They never had. In 1794 their presence was reported simultaneously in both a cheap lodging house in Boston and the best tavern in Philadelphia.[9] Tiffin & Son, 'Bug Destroyers to Her Majesty', would have been spoiled for opportunities with many parts of London overrun with bugs, although in practice they limited themselves to one hundred clients, auctioning vacancies when they became available. In 1801 Johann Heinrich Jördens assembled all the bedbug knowledge then extant, largely by copying Southall's text unacknowledged. (This resembles the practice currently employed for many bedbug

'fact sheets' found on the Internet.) Jördens wrote that 'in no way does the bedbug occur more frequently in the huts of the poor than in the many-arcaded palaces of the larger towns.'[10]

The bedbug is now found in shelters and five-star hotels, in luxury homes and brothels, in military barracks and residential homes, in hospitals and family homes, in camper vans and shops, on trains and in zoos. The myth of an association with poverty, poor hygiene and lower class, however, is as ineradicable as the bedbug itself. I believe that a stunningly simple reason is

Ronald Ginther, 'Looking for Bedbugs', 1936. From the series *The Great Depression*.

Through decades and centuries, bedbugs have had an unproven association with filth and unhygienic conditions of any kind, resulting in this bedbug rating a run-down room five stars.

Bedbug Hotel Reviews

responsible: there are more cheap hostels, small lodging houses and family apartments than five-star hotels and villas. In addition, it can be imagined that the owners of the latter may be in a better position to pay out six-figure sums for out-of-court compensation, well before reports of bug occurrences might be published online.

The poor also have less money to publish about bugs or point the finger at others. It is interesting to speculate what would have happened to the status of the bedbug if literature had not been dominated for centuries by the rich. Would bedbugs have become a symbol of prosperity, had poorer people filled fiction with their experiences of them while working in the houses of the rich as cleaners, kitchen helps and children's maids?

For the poor it must also be more difficult to refuse a newspaper's financial offer to have a photograph taken, and later globally distributed, showing bedbug bites on a leg or other body part, thereby reinforcing the vicious circle that views poverty, bedbugs and poor hygiene as synonymous.

Shrewsbury, who advertised his full academic history on the title page of his book in a way that only medical doctors do, associates the bedbugs 'with slum conditions of dilapidation, squalor, alcoholism, and neglect of personal hygiene', even though he admits shortly after that it is not only the overcrowded and poorer areas of cities and towns that are affected, and that bedbugs are also present in new housing estates and in better-class houses.[11] Shrewsbury, of course, emphasized that he, the writer, lived a life miles away from dilapidation, squalor, alcoholism and neglect of personal hygiene. His next depiction of the Other is more specific: Scotland Road in Liverpool, 'probably one of the worst slum areas in Europe' and inhabited by improvident and intemperate Irish. It seems that Shrewsbury adores providence and temperance, but he would not explain how or why these qualities would keep bedbugs away.

It may well be that the poor are more often associated with bedbugs than the rich, but that is simply because there are many more poor than rich in the world. When the fact that the poor have fewer opportunities to cover up any infestations is taken into consideration, it seems clear that bedbugs may have little to do with poverty, just with numbers.

Blaming the lower social classes for the miseries of society or the ravages of disease effectively creates a different depiction of the Other that is by no means restricted to the past. In today's Germany, for example, it is not uncommon to speak of, and perhaps even more common to think of, recipients of social benefits as parasites, or more delicately as *Sozialschmarotzer*, parasites of the social system. David Cameron's reference to a 'swarm of immigrants' at Calais probably comes next in the row. Sometimes it feels as if it may not be too long before certain politicians start speaking in public about blood-sucking or bedbugs.

That the poor may also use bedbugs to point out their social disadvantages does nothing to dismantle the maintenance of the poor Other. In *The Harp in the South* Ruth Park describes how it was traditional at New Year to burn old clothes and paper along with their many bedbugs, but Dolour's poor family 'had little to burn at all, for they wore all their old clothes, and used their old newspapers as packing for their beds in winter, as newspaper is warmer than blankets and doesn't require washing'. Her sister Roie asks, 'And who would pay for the cyanide fumigation. Not the landlord; he got his rent even if his property were vermin-infested.'[12] There is indeed the issue that pest control costs money. After Jane Carlyle found bedbugs in her house in October 1849, she instantly realized that tearing down the curtains and sending them 'to the dyers, not so much to have the colour renewed, as to have the bugs boiled to death', was 'an immense expense'.

Distorted perspectives on bedbugs can also be found in the reports of German prisoners of war after their return home. In many First World War and post-war memoirs and diaries 'the Russian' is presented as being infested with lice and living in houses that were breeding sites for the worst bedbug infestations. The not so dissimilar bedbug situations current in Berlin and other large German cities were ignored. The subtle way in which this belief in one's superiority crept into the mind, perhaps unconsciously, can also be seen in Albrecht Hase's research papers. He describes farmhouses abandoned by those who had fled from the German army in such a hurry that they had not even taken their bedding with them. Hase put the buildings to use as laboratories and experimented with sulphurous acid, 'because at the time there did not seem to be any point in trying to prevent damage to the rooms'.[13]

We have seen that bedbugs are an obvious target to shoulder the burden of the Other, because they destroy our daily comfort by sucking blood and live secluded lives in large groups, appearing suddenly out of nowhere and leaving an unpleasant smell. Other factors that may contribute to this sense of Other include an intrinsic fear of ectoparasites. Some researchers suggest that a fear of small, light brown, flat objects – resembling lice, bedbugs and fleas, but not so much ticks – is imprinted biologically, per-haps even in our genes. This genetic fear may have proved an advantage in the past to help avoid diseases. These ideas are speculative, but it is true that while eight or nine people out of ten guess incorrectly when shown a bedbug, many at least assume that they have been shown some kind of dangerous insect or parasite. Experiments with schoolchildren have shown similar results.

Another suggestion of an intense but learned response to avoiding dangerous creatures by invoking feelings of disgust can be observed when talking about bedbugs. I, of course, like talk-ing about bedbugs and do so very often. I am amazed how many people then start to scratch themselves lightly and uncon-sciously. When asked about it, many admit that they get goose pimples or their hairs stand on end – a physical sign of disgust. May I confess that even I still experience this unconscious need to scratch, as a press photographer recently pointed out (and documented). Since I cannot imagine that anybody talks about bedbugs more than I, and so should be able to resist the urge, the scratching seems a pretty robust response. And while writing this, I cannot help wondering how many readers are actually scratching themselves, feeling a shiver or getting goose pimples.

9 Bugging Forecast: Unknown, Disliked, Occasionally Intimate

Why such hatred for fundamentally harmless pests –
these tiny, non-disease carrying, functionally invisible insects?
Ben Winters, *Bedbugs* (2011)

We have seen in Chapter Four that conflicts between two parties can be solved in three ways: avoidance, resistance and tolerance. Humans have tried to avoid bedbugs and it has helped in some cases (see Chapter Seven), but since bedbugs are still able to find us, success seems incomplete. A second solution is to fight bedbugs. Humans have put huge efforts into this, but their continuing presence indicates that this trick hasn't worked perfectly either. Even worse, resistance appears to work both ways, and we now have resistant bedbugs. Nearly all past attempts have failed to get rid of bedbugs in a certain region, to keep their numbers down or keep them out of dwellings permanently. They have proven to be here to stay: 'it stands to reason you won't never have no bugs', as Mumma says in *The Harp in the South*, just as Roie 'had been squashing bugs all her life'.[1] The bugs were abhorred, but slowly lost their alien nature.

At some stage in a conflict one party may realize that being tough on the other costs more than it is actually worth. In this case, the third option is to accept the other's presence and get on with your life. What? *Tolerating* bedbugs? This sounds awkward – we can't be soft on them, can we? We have to fight them, don't we? Sheldon Lou describes how in communist China the suggestion of peaceful coexistence with bedbugs could only have come from some bourgeois 'backward elements'. Bedbugs, or 'bedbug warriors', which were equipped with nothing, not even a brain, were fought 'with Chairman Mao's thought and heavy chemical weapons', confident 'that eliminating bedbugs would be a walk in the park'.[2] After years of fighting, though, the tormented gave in and tried tolerance, perhaps in an echo of the Buddhist tradition in China. Sheldon Lou even expresses sympathy towards the tormentors: 'I dream I'm surrounded by millions of bedbugs . . . Some even come out from inside me. But I feel I deserve it – the penalty for killing too many bedbugs.'[3]

The toleration of bedbugs is painful physically, but may pay off in terms of mental relaxation. Humans seem to have tried that too, or at least they may have had no choice. The painful bit is still there, but are we about to approach the relaxing bit?

The first delicate signs of some degree of acceptance of the bedbug enemy have already been presented in previous chapters in the form of English and African proverbs. Some acceptance may also be seen in the Swiss author Gottfried Keller's sympathetic description of the bedbug as 'the good beastie', or Dionysus' earlier mentioned request in Aristophanes' play *The Frogs* for a hostel with 'fewer' bugs.

The Other is gradually becoming normalized and familiar to humans. The bedbugs in the Hopi tales are ordinary creatures with mothers and fathers, wives, aunts and children. They even have – the crown of normality – marital arguments. In *La Grande Symphonie héroïque des punaises* a couple of bugs elicit our empathy because they are expecting a baby. However, they have to separate because the male is being drafted for a great battle on a tired traveller. In a recent e-book bedbugs are the only comfort and confidants to a boy suffering from abuse at home.[4]

A less radical acceptance of bedbugs is shown by their friendly appearance in cartoons. One may even slowly begin to joke about

Another renaissance of bedbug acceptance? A cuddly toy of a bedbug of about 20 cm in length with large, beautiful eyes, somewhat unusual mouthparts and the correct number of legs.

bedbugs. It is perhaps no coincidence that most bedbug cartoons online are in English, running parallel to the fact that over the past fifteen years increases in bedbug infestations have been particularly found in the English-speaking world – the UK, U.S., Australia and Canada. Bedbug jokes are becoming acceptable since there is always someone being pestered daily with pictures of apartment infestations, or who has been bitten or heard of a hotel that has bedbugs. This is no longer news, but it was the same in the last century when bugs and their associated jokes were thriving.

Eventually, the funny, and not so funny, cartoons will have their day. Bedbugs will become a larger part of our daily lives, and not just in the form of wall pins or electronic devices. Today they appear on T-shirts ('I bug N.Y.'), they are talked about, and even bedbug games and toys are being sold. One of the most precious items in my collection is a golden amulet (yes, golden!) in the shape of a bed, the bedframe of which can be popped out to reveal a bedbug sitting on it. Even though I have no idea who would want to wear it, a bedbug amulet is quite a demonstration of the normalization of bedbugs. If, over time, the normalization of bedbugs continues, they may leave a mark in names and places. Otsego, in New York state, has a Bedbug Hill Road, where of all things there is a bed and breakfast at number 434. Just 100 km (62 mi.) to the west, in Pennsylvania, alongside Bedbug Brook, runs Bed Bug Hollow Road. The Austrian town of Weiz has a

A golden amulet. An undated piece of small jewellery (approximately 2 cm) showing a bedbug underneath a bed. The inset shows the bedbug is clearly recognizable even though the number of segments is too large and there is a clear furrow along the body.

An old postcard depicting Bedbug Island in Lake Hopatcong, New Jersey.

BED BUG ISLAND BY MOONLIGHT, LAKE HOPATCONG, N. J.

Wanzenweg, while the people of Oberlauringen in Franconia (Bavaria) are lucky enough to have a Wanzengasse ('bug lane'). Moving to France, there is a Chemin des Punaises in the commune of Sciez, across the border from Geneva, and a Ruelle Punaise in the Old Town of Lyon. In Vex, in the Swiss Alps near Sion, there is a farmhouse called Les Punaises. In Peru, northeast of Lima, there is a mountain called Chinche, and a town and district called Chinchero. A little island in Lake Hopatcong in New Jersey has been named after the bedbug and is quite a romantic place ('itching to get there' has not been used in advertisements, though). By contrast, back in France, the car shop called Cimex-Services in Chartres and the C.i.m.e.x. trading company in Saint-Cyprien may not have chosen their acronyms in full understanding of the meaning.

Further evidence for the transition of bedbugs from being the Other to integrating with society comes from their place among the most commonly used remedies in medieval times in Chinese and European herbal books.[5] In order to be a useful remedy, however, they had to be something different or uncommon: anything too common would probably have been perceived as having no curative effect. Pulverized bedbugs were reportedly very good

> to provoke Urine, to expel Birth, and after Birth. Seven of them swallowed before the Fit approacheth, cure the Quartan Ague, as Diascorides testifies. The stinking smell which proceedeth from them, cures the suffocation of the Matrix. Four being taken three mornings in wine, cure the colic . . . Pulverized, and mixt with the oil of Roses, and honey, they cure the pains of ears . . . pulverized and taken in any fit Vehicle, they cure Fevers, and the spitting of blood.[6]

Dioscorides recommended mixing them with tortoise blood or attaching them to the left arm with stolen sheep's wool.[7]

If God is almighty, bedbugs must have a purpose. Carthusian monks believed that the divine role of the bedbug was that of an alarm clock, following the arguments of the Greek Stoic philosopher Chrysippus. This gives another meaning to the piercing call of the alarm clock, and seems to reflect the successful ability of bedbugs to disturb sleepers.

Even the bizarre mating habits of bedbugs have made a transition into normality. A homeopathic remedy based on bedbugs promises to cure ovarian pain, but only in the left ovary![8] This homoeopathic practitioner seems to have studied bedbug traumatic insemination more thoroughly than medicine (even though in the bedbug it is the right side that is traumatically inseminated – 'with pain' – because left and right in biology is assigned as if looking from the body, not at the body). We will now find that the bedbug has experienced other peculiar normalizations.

The bedbug's flatness allegedly helped Albert Einstein to explain how an ultrathin, non-transparent entity without volume could throw a shadow into infinity.[9] Here is how: the ultrathin bedbug walks along a glass globe, which is illuminated from the North Pole. As it walks from the south towards the North Pole, it throws a slowly growing shadow onto a piece of paper placed below the globe. At the moment when the bug is directly on the North Pole, the shadow flips and becomes infinite.

Europeans could also have learned from the Chinese. If they had read more thoroughly a specific chapter from the herbal book *Bencao gangmu* (1578), they would not have had to wait another hundred years for Francesco Redi to disprove Aristotle's assertion that pests reproduce spontaneously from the dust. It clearly states that bedbug eggs are laid, from which nymphs are hatched. Indeed, Thomas Muffet had also mentioned in his *Theatrum insectorum* (published posthumously in 1634) that bedbugs 'propagate by copulation' and provided observations of bedbug eggs, nymphs and adults in the scabbard of a sword.

Amazingly, the bedbug can serve to promote good manners. In France they are used to bite one's tongue instead of swearing (*pu . . . naise*), which is similar to the English 's . . . ugar'. Finally, bedbugs can be helpful for rebuilding relationships with somewhat neglected mothers-in-law. I recently received an email detailing the result of a bedbug infestation: 'We are forced to move out of our home and are taking refuge in my parents-in-law's house. So, the bedbug problem beats the horror of living with your in-laws!' What an appreciation!

Imagine the loss of economic growth we would face without bed-bugs. We have already seen how nourishing the idea of the bug as a scary and current threat increases sales in musical tickets and books, the flourishing of pest control companies and, therefore, the continuation of bedbug research.

Of the thousands of pest control companies worldwide, a substantial number in cities in the u.s. and uk have exclusively specialized in bedbug control. Bedbugs are big business.

There are smaller research labs working on nothing but bed-bugs. There are now companies specializing in breeding and selling live bedbugs to provide educational material for pest controllers, hotel staff, the sniffer dog trainers and whoever else needs bedbug education. Smartphone applications are being developed in which the information is much more hands-on than the large educational wall posters from the 1930s. Other businesses thrive more indirectly from the bug's reputation. A variant of the Borgward iv, a remote-controlled German tank used in the Second World War, was known as the Wanze (Bedbug) when equipped with six anti-tank rockets; scale-model kits are available for purchase by model-makers. The name has also been given to a lawn mower: perhaps the flat, sturdy and robust nature of the bedbug, which moves forward no matter what lies ahead, has positive connotations. If there were no bedbugs, the resulting economic losses would be heavy for the writers and publishers of books advising how to get rid of bedbugs: kill, eradicate, avoid, control, eliminate or any other means of disposal. Hundreds of such books have been published within the last decade, together with dozens of children's books.

More seriously, one may perhaps see the bedbug as a decisive originator of the very existence of household pest control services,

An advertising comic strip telling the story of a couple whose peace and love is disturbed by bedbugs until the housewife finds the right remedy in a nearby drugstore. These comics have been used widely for advertising bug-killing substances, and have certainly helped to promote the popularity of comics.

although this is my hypothesis, not a proven fact. Fleas, lice and other 'pests' are unlikely to cause such strong responses, because they don't live in the household per se. However, bedbugs are sufficiently housebound to have inspired pest control businesses, with, perhaps, a little assistance from rats and cockroaches.

Along with pest control came the advertising for it. The head of the Tiffin family firm, well aware of the significance of public opinion and attention, told Henry Mayhew in the 1850s:

Heinrich Zille, *Bug Hunt*, c. 1910. The Berlin-based milieu painter captures the moment when children are busy catching bedbugs. Here, Zille chose to present a connection of bedbugs to poverty and prostitution. The sign on the wall reads: The Lord is my Shepherd.

I thought I must have something over my shop, that would be . . . suitable . . . to my business; so I had a transparency done, and stretched a big frame, and lit up by gas, on which was written – 'May the destroyers of peace be destroyed by us, Tiffin & Son, bug-destroyers to Her Majesty.'[10]

As a transparency, this might have been one of the first ever illuminated advertisements – thank you, bedbug. Other transparency advertisements would soon follow, although modern bedbug controllers did not use the same tactics until many years later.

Tiffin also went for an approach that might be one of the earliest cases of comparative advertising: 'my work is . . . scientific treating of the bugs rather than wholesale murder. We don't care about the thousands, it's the last bug we look for, whilst your carpenters and upholsterers leave as many behind them, perhaps, as they manage to catch.'[11]

Advertisements for bedbug control had further consequences, some of which have persisted to the present day: for example, John Southall, the first bedbug controller to advertise his services publicly, already felt the need to introduce and advertise a warranty: 'If he in any ways damages the Furniture, he will pay for the same.'[12] Advertisements later evolved, sometimes closely linked to the development and distribution of comic strips. Cartoons showing bedbug-killing remedies became particularly popular in the 1930s.

In one case of bedbugs providing economic advantage, described in Robert Swanson's *Rhymes of a Lumberjack* (1943), a single bedbug found someone a job. It crawled out of the interviewee's coat and helped alleviate the tense atmosphere in the interview. It then walked across the sparkling clean desk, generating a shared sense of a common enemy that resulted in the interviewee being hired.

To summarize, the bedbug can be useful. For our own peace of mind, let us try to tolerate bugs in our lives by adopting their names for wall pins, computer bugs and anything else that bugs you but is of minor significance. Let us tolerate them as occasional blood suckers (at least they don't make that high-pitched mosquito sound – wouldn't that make a good start for making peace with them?), as something that makes you see your in-laws in a different light, as something we have to control and study, and as something we won't win a war against anyway.

Given that a major problem of keeping bug numbers low is insecticide resistance, we may need more imaginative solutions than letting every pest controller use their own pesticides in their own way, or simply calling for new pesticides (to which bedbugs, in turn, will soon evolve resistance), or even calling for the return of old ones, such as DDT. We had better get along with bedbugs somehow: we have to, as they won't ask us. And perhaps we are already making progress in accepting them. This may be apparent not only in the rising number of bedbug-related cartoons and jokes but in the fact that the first question asked by a pest controller when called to an infestation is no longer: 'Have you recently been on holiday *abroad*?'

There may be individual preferences regarding when such a tolerance towards bedbugs should end and when resistance should take over. Should this be when too many e-bugs have been installed into our homes, streets, cars and telephones? Or when Internet cookies are openly called *bugs* to express what they actually are, electronic spying devices violating personal freedom? Or when naming the Other promotes racist and anti-humanist expression?

Without the bedbug we would be missing something. No longer would we have a culprit that could be blamed for transmitting every newly emerging disease, or a fitting name to adopt for our enemies or anything that is different to us. We would also lack, perhaps even miss, medical curiosities, incredible biological facts that creationists would have trouble explaining, as Jeremy Hardy joked in BBC Radio 4's *News Quiz*, or something to name anything that doesn't work. On top of that, the bedbug starred in an entire episode of *The Simpsons*. Thank you, Bedbug, for all of this. Can we start tolerating it somehow? Not that I wish to volunteer . . .

La Punaise
—

Dans l'ombre, odorante punaise,
Tu fuis dans les fentes du lit,
Et toute la nuit à ton aise
Tu nous dévores sans répit.
La petite femme en chemise
Qui, dans de gracieux décors,
Te poursuit, montrant ses trésors,
O punaise, te poétise !
                Armand GABORIAUD.

Detail from a saucy French postcard of *c.* 1905 showing a woman in alluring night dress, with a frivolous poem. This illustration shows that the not-so-rare association of bedbugs with female eroticism is not a product of modern society.

The words of the psalmist, 'thou shalt not need to be afrayed for eny bugges by night', as translated in the Coverdale Bible of 1535, brings me to the end of this journey. I am delighted to have reached it without mentioning the most commonly repeated and worn-out phrase about bedbugs: 'Goodnight, don't let . . .'.

Timeline of the Bedbug

100 MILLION BP	800,000–100,000 BP	c. 1350 BC	LATE 5TH CENTURY BC
The earliest known bedbug-like features appear on an example of *Quasicimex* embedded in mid-Cretaceous amber	Possible evolution of the first bedbugs specialized to live on humans	Bedbugs present in the workmen's village at Tell el-Amana, Egypt	Bedbugs mentioned by Aristophanes as living in bed pallets (*The Clouds*, 423 BC) and hostels (*The Frogs*, 405 BC)

1578	1583	1645	1730
Bedbugs are described in the Chinese herbal book *Ben Cao Kang Mu* as laying eggs, disproving Aristotle's idea of spontaneous regeneration 100 years before Francesco Redi's *Osservazioni* (1684)	Bedbugs reported in London	John Evelyn reports from Italy on the benefits of metal-framed beds against bedbugs	John Southall publishes *A Treatise of Buggs*

1930S	1930–41	1946	1966	1982
London and Berlin have urban quarters that are 100 per cent infested with bedbugs	Heyday of bedbug research: Kenneth Mellanby and Cecil George Johnson in England; Albrecht Hase and Heinrich Kemper in Germany	Bedbugs evolve resistance to DDT, five years after its initial introduction	Publication of Robert Usinger's *A Monograph of Cimicidae*	Publication of Clive Sinclair's short story 'Bedbugs'

c. 350 BC	2ND/3RD CENTURY AD	c. 1000	1568
Bedbugs mentioned by Aristotle	Bedbugs living at a Romano-British site in Warwickshire, England	Anglo-Saxons share their privacy with bedbugs in Norfolk	First specific depiction of a bedbug-infested bed in Pietro Andrea Mattioli's *Discorsi*

1748	1913	1915	1920	1929
Pehr Kalm reports that bedbugs are common on the east coast of North America	First correct interpretation of the traumatic copulation habits of the bedbug by Patton and Cragg	Franz Kafka's *Die Verwandlung* (The Metamorphosis) is published	The bedbug is among the first three insects on which Zyklon, later to become Zyklon B, is tested	Premiere of Mayakovsky's play *The Bedbug* in Moscow on 13 February

1992	2000	2001	2011	2014	2016
Bernard Werber's *Le Jour des fourmis* portrays bedbugs as horrible sex machines	Bedbugs are established as a major problem in large Western cities	Bedbugs become a model system for biology research	Ben Winters's novel *Bedbugs* appears, playing on people's horror of bedbugs	The musical *Bedbugs!!!* sells out off-Broadway	The bedbug genome deciphered by two different research groups

References

1 BUG DIVERSITY

1 Klaus Reinhardt et al., 'Who Knows the Bedbug? Knowledge of Adult Bedbug Appearance Increases with People's Age in Three Counties of Great Britain', *Journal of Medical Entomology*, XLV/5 (2008), pp. 956–8; Conrad Seidel and Klaus Reinhardt, 'Bugging Forecast: Unknown, Disliked, Occasionally Intimate. Bed Bugs in Germany Meet Unprepared People', *PLOS ONE*, VIII (2013), article no. e51083.

2 Klaus Reinhardt, *Literarische Wanzen: Eine Anthologie: Nebst einer kleinen Natur- und Kulturgeschichte* (Berlin, 2014).

3 Robert Leslie Usinger, *Monograph of Cimicidae* (Washington, DC, 1966).

4 Ondrej Balvin et al., 'Mitochondrial DNA and Morphology Show Independent Evolutionary Histories of Bedbug *Cimex lectularius* (Heteroptera: Cimicidae) on Bats and Humans', *Parasitology Research*, CXI/1 (2012), pp. 457–69.

5 Ibid.

6 Herbert Weidner, 'Die Entstehung der Hausinsekten', *Zeitschrift für Angewandte Entomologie*, XLII (1958), pp. 429–47.

7 Richard C. Axtell, 'Poultry Integrated Pest Management: Status and Future', *Integrated Pest Management Reviews*, IV/1 (1999), pp. 53–73.

2 BUG YEARS

1 Eva Panagiotakopulu and Paul C. Buckland, '*Cimex lectularius* L.', the Common Bed Bug from Pharaonic Egypt', *Antiquity*, LXXIII (1999), pp. 908–11.

2 Edith Schmidt, 'Käferreste aus dem Sarg der ottonischen Königin Editha (910–946): Schädlinge aus der Grablege von 946 und Laufkäfer aus der Umbettung von 1510', *Archäologie in Sachsen-Anhalt*, Sonderband XVIII (2012), pp. 207–44.

3 Friedrich S. Bodenheimer, *Materialien zur Geschichte der Entomologie bis Linné*, vol. I (Berlin, 1928).

4 Chuo Io, *A History of Chinese Entomology* (Beijing, 1990), p. 137.

5 Jacob Grimm and Wilhelm Grimm, 'Wanze', in *Deutsches Wörterbuch*, vol. XXVII (Munich, 2010), p. 1926.

6 'Coverdale Bible', https://en.wikipedia.org/wiki/Bible_errata, accessed 17 February 2016.

7 L.O.J. Boynton, 'The Bed-bug and the "Age of Elegance"', *Furniture History*, I (1963), pp. 13–31.

8 Peter Quennell, ed., *Mayhew's London: Selections from London Labour and the London Poor* (London, 1949), p. 430; Boynton, 'The Bed-bug', p. 21.

9 Klaus Reinhardt, 'Pesets'ola: Which Bed Bug Did the Hopi Know? (A Present for Robert Leslie Usinger's 100th Birthday)', *American Entomologist*, LVIII (2012), pp. 58–9.

10 Nadar and Charles Bataille, *La Grande Symphonie héroïque des punaises* (Paris, 1877).

11 Ministry of Health, *Report on the Bed-bug* (London, 1933), p. 4.

12 Heinrich Kemper, 'Die Bettwanze und ihre Bekämpfung', *Hygienische Zoologie*, IV (1936), pp. 1–107.

13 Theodor Fontane, *Aus England und Schottland* (Munich, 1963), p. 534.

14 Ernst Haeckel, *Berg- und Seereisen 1857/1883*, ed. H. Schmidt (Leipzig, 1913); Klaus Reinhardt, 'Ein bisher unbekannter Erstnachweis der Bettwanze für die Insel Lanzarote – 1866 durch Ernst Haeckel', *Entomologische Nachrichten und Berichte*, LI (2007), pp. 52–3.

15 Alexandre Dumas, *Reise im Kaukasus, 1858–1859*, ed. G.F.W. Rödiger (Pest, 1859).

16 Anton Tschechow, *Die Insel Sachalin* (Zürich, 1976), p. 69.

17 George Kennan, . . . *und der Zar ist weit: Sibirien 1885* (Berlin, 1981), p. 271.

18 J. R. Phelps, 'Eradication of Vermin on Board Ship', *United States Naval Medical Bulletin*, xx (1924), pp. 256–64.

19 May Berenbaum, *Bugs in the System: Insects and their Impact on Human Affairs* (New York, 1995).

20 Ruth Bondy, 'Frauen in Theresienstadt und im Familienlager in Auschwitz-Birkenau', in *Frauen im Holocaust*, ed. Barbara Distel (Gerlingen, 2001), p. 129.

21 For southern Africa, see K. Newberry and E. J. Jansen, 'The Common Bedbug *Cimex lectularius* in African Huts', *Transactions of the Royal Society of Tropical Medicine and Hygiene*, LXXX (1986), pp. 653–8; for Malawi, see Brian Morris, *Insects and Human Life* (Oxford, 2004).

22 Conrad Seidel and Klaus Reinhardt, 'Bugging Forecast: Unknown, Disliked, Occasionally Intimate. Bed Bugs in Germany Meet Unprepared People', *PLOS ONE*, VIII (2013), article no. e51083.

3 BUG LIFE

1 Eileen Harris, *Going to Bed* (London, 1981).

2 Hans Ostwald, *Das Zillebuch* (Berlin, 1929), p. 384.

3 Ruth Park, *The Harp in the South* (Sydney, 1948).

4 Ezekiel Rivnay, 'Studies in Tropisms of the Bed Bug *Cimex lectularius* L.', *Parasitology*, xxiv (1932), pp. 121–36.

5 As mentioned by J.F.D. Shrewsbury, *The Plague of the Philistines, and Other Medical-historical Essays* (London, 1964), p. 156.

6 Park, *Harp in the South*, p. 115.

7 E.N.I. Weeks et al., 'A Bioassay for Studying Behavioural Responses of the Common Bed Bug, *Cimex lectularius* (Hemiptera: Cimicidae) to Bed Bug-derived Volatiles', *Bulletin of Entomological Research*, CI (2011), pp. 1–8.

8 Sheldon Lou, *Sparrows, Bedbugs, and Body Shadows: A Memoir* (Honolulu, HI, 2005), p. 90.

9 Heinrich Kemper, *Die tierischen Schädlinge im Sprachgebrauch* (Berlin, 1959).

10 'The Thing (Listening Device)', https://en.wikipedia.org, accessed 18 August 2016.

11 Park, *Harp in the South*, p. 15.

12 Henry Mayhew, cited in L.O.J. Boynton, 'The Bed-bug and the "Age of Elegance"', *Furniture History*, I (1963), p. 16.

13 Ekkehart Malotki, ed., *The Bedbugs' Night Dance and Other Hopi Tales of Sexual Encounter* (Lincoln, NE, 1997).

14 Sheldon Lou, *Sparrows*, p. 92.

15 Ben Winters, *Bedbugs* (Philadelphia, PA, 2011).

16 Joseph M. Piel, 'Der portugiesische Name der Wanze: *percevejo*, ein etymologisches Rätsel?', *Zeitschrift für romanische Philologie*, CII/5–6 (1985), pp. 491–2.

17 Park, *Harp in the South*, p. 15.

18 Clive Sinclair, 'Bedbugs', in *Bedbugs* (London, 1982), p. 9.

19 Winters, *Bedbugs*, p. 141.

20 Paul Heller, 'Kafka, Franz. Die Verwandlung', in *Kindlers Neues Literatur-Lexikon*, ed. Walter Jens (Munich, 2000).

21 Gottfried Keller, *Die Leute von Seldwyla* (Berlin, 1976), pp. 250–51.

22 Sinclair, 'Bedbugs', p. 9.

23 Winters, *Bedbugs*, p. 157.

24 Jerome Goddard and Richard de Shazo, 'Psychological Effects of Bed Bug Attacks (*Cimex lectularius* L.)', *American Journal of Medicine*, CXXV (2012), pp. 101–3. For the quote, see Winters, *Bedbugs*, p. 190.

25 Toby Fountain et al., 'Human-facilitated Metapopulation Dynamics in an Emerging Pest Species, *Cimex lectularius*', *Molecular Ecology*, XXIII/5 (2015), pp. 1071–84.

26 Klaus Reinhardt and Anne-Cécile Ribou, 'Females Become Infertile as the Stored Sperm's Oxygen Radicals Increase', *Scientific Reports*, III (2013), article no. 2888.

4 BUG SEX: REAL AND IN FICTION

1 Klaus Reinhardt, Nils Anthes and Rolanda Lange, 'Copulatory Wounding and Traumatic Insemination', in *Sexual Conflict*, ed. W. R. Rice and S. Gavrilets (Cold Spring Harbor, NY, 2015), pp. 115–40.

2 Ibid.

3 Edward H. Morrow and Göran Arnqvist, 'Costly Traumatic Insemination and a Female Counter-adaptation in Bed Bugs', *Proceedings of the Royal Society, Biological Series*, CCLXX (2003), pp. 2377–81; Klaus Reinhardt, Richard Naylor and Michael T. Siva-Jothy, 'Reducing a Cost of Traumatic Insemination: Female Bedbugs Evolve a Unique Organ', *Proceedings of the Royal Society, Biological Series*, CCLXX (2003), pp. 2371–5.

4 Jan Michels, Stanislav Gorb and Klaus Reinhardt, 'Reduction of Female Copulatory Damage by Resilin Represents Evidence for Tolerance in Sexual Conflict', *Journal of the Royal Society Interface*, XII (2015), article no. 20141107.

5 Clive Sinclair, 'Bedbugs', in *Bedbugs* (London, 1982), p. 9.

6 Rowan Hooper, 'Bugs Turn Transsexual to Avoid Stabbing Penises', *New Scientist*, 19 September 2007, p. 11.

7 Andrew B. Barron and Mark J. F. Brown, 'Science Journalism: Let's Talk About Sex', *Nature*, CDLXXXVIII (2012), pp. 151–2.

8 'Bedbug', *Seduce Me* (dir. Isabella Rossellini, 2010), www.sundance. tv, accessed 19 May 2013.

9 Klaus Reinhardt, 'Pesets'ola: Which Bed Bug Did the Hopi Know? (A Present for Robert Leslie Usinger's 100th Birthday)', *American Entomologist*, LVIII (2012), pp. 58–9.

10 Ekkehart Malotki, ed., *The Bedbugs' Night Dance and Other Hopi Tales of Sexual Encounter* (Lincoln, NE, 1997).

11 Iona Opie and Peter Opie, *The Lore and Language of Schoolchildren* (Oxford, 1959).

12 R. Hoeppli and I. Chiang, 'The Louse, Crab-louse and Bedbug in Old Chinese Medical Literature with Special Consideration on Phtiriasis', *Chinese Medical Journal*, LVIII (1940), pp. 338–62.

5 ITCHING TO SUCCEED

1 C. Hay Murray, 'Notes on the Anatomy of the Bed Bug, *(Acanthia) lectularia* L.', *Parasitology*, VII/3 (1914), pp. 278–321; I. M. Puri, 'Studies on the Anatomy of *Cimex lectularius* L.', *Parasitology*, XVI (1924), p. 86.
2 Ibid., p. 89.
3 Ibid., pp. 91–2.
4 Raymond E. Ryckman, 'Dermatological Reactions to the Bites of Four Species of Triatominae (Hemiptera: Reduviidae) and *Cimex lectularius* L. (Hemiptera: Cimicidae)', *Bulletin of the Society for Vector Ecology*, X (1985), pp. 122–5.

6 BUG DARE

1 Ben Winters, *Bedbugs* (Philadelphia, PA, 2011).
2 Alexandre Arsène Girault, 'The Bedbug, *Cimex lectularius* Linnaeus, Pt. IIb. Critical Remarks on its Literature, with a History and Bibliography of Pathogenic Relations', *Psyche*, XI (1905), pp. 42–3.
3 Klaus Reinhardt, 'The Entomological Institute of the Waffen-SS: Evidence for Offensive Biological Warfare Research in the Third Reich', *Endeavour*, XXXVII (2013), pp. 220–27.

7 DECLARING WAR ON BUGS

1 Ministry of Health, *Report on the Bed-bug* (London, 1933), p. 10.
2 Brooke Borrel, *Infested: How the Bed Bug Infiltrated Our Bedrooms and Took Over the World* (Chicago, IL, 2015), p. 164.
3 L.O.J. Boynton, 'The Bed-bug and the "Age of Elegance"', *Furniture History*, I (1963), p. 17.
4 Ibid.
5 Jacob Grimm and Wilhelm Grimm, 'Wanze', in *Deutsches Wörterbuch*, vol. XXVII (Munich, 2010), p. 1928.
6 Eugen Strouhal, *Life in Ancient Egypt* (Cambridge, 1992), p. 74.

7 Hans-Joachim Hoffmann, 'Ernstes und Kurioses über Wanzen – ein Heteropterologisches Panoptikum', *Denisia*, xix (2006), pp. 95–136.

8 Boynton, 'The Bed-bug', p. 21.

9 Kurt Tucholsky, 'Deutsches Chaos', *Die Weltbühne*, xxxi (1931), p. 179.

10 G. K. Maurice, 'The Entry of Elapsing Fever into the Sudan', *Sudan Notes and Records*, xv (1932), p. 105.

11 Boynton, 'The Bed-bug', p. 17.

12 Stefan von Bogdandy, 'Ausrottung von Bettwanzen mit Bohnenblättern', *Die Naturwissenschaften*, xv (1927), p. 474.

13 H. H. Richardson, 'The Action of Bean Leaves Against the Bedbug', *Journal of Economic Entomology*, xxxvi (1943), pp. 543–5.

14 Ruth Marx, 'Über die Wirtsfindung und die Bedeutung des artspezifischen Duftstoffes bei *Cimex lectularius* Linné', *Zeitschrift für Parasitenkunde*, xvii (1955), p. 44.

15 Megan W. Szyndler et al., 'Entrapment of Bed Bugs by Leaf Trichomes Inspires Microfabrication of Biomimetic Surfaces', *Journal of the Royal Society Interface*, x (2013), article no. 20130174.

16 Lawrence Wright, *Warm and Snug: The History of the Bed* (London, 1962).

17 E. A. Temu et al., 'Bedbug Control by Permethrin-impregnated Bednets in Tanzania', *Medical and Veterinary Entomology*, xiii (1999), pp. 457–9.

18 Lee Brown, 'Children's Decoration Tips', *Interiordezine*, 23 August 2011, www.interiordezine.com, accessed 17 February 2016.

19 Wright, *Warm and Snug*, p. 3.

20 Fyodor Dostoyevsky, *Aufzeichnungen aus einem Totenhause* (Leipzig, 1999), p. 274.

21 Dr Blau, 'Die Planmäßige Insektenbekämpfung bei den Russen', *Zeitschrift für Hygiene und Infektionskrankheiten*, lxxxiii (1917), pp. 346–52.

22 Klaus Reinhardt, *Literarische Wanzen: Eine Anthologie. Nebst einer Kleinen Natur- und Kulturgeschichte* (Berlin, 2014).

23 Eileen Harris, *Going to Bed* (London, 1981), p. 46.

24 Ibid., p. 30.
25 Wright, *Warm and Snug*, p. 237.
26 Boynton, 'The Bed-bug', p. 25.
27 Ibid., p. 13.
28 Anonymous, *The Bed-bug: Its Habits and Life History and How to Deal with It* (London, 1954).
29 Wright, *Warm and Snug*, p. 166; Harris, *Going to Bed*.
30 Richard Naylor and Clive Boase, 'Practical Solutions for Treating Laundry Infested with *Cimex lectularius* (Hemiptera: Cimicidae)', *Journal of Economic Entomology*, CIII (2010), pp. 136–9.
31 Boynton, 'The Bed-bug', p. 26.
32 James R. Busvine, *Insects and Hygiene* (London, 1966), p. 67.
33 Johann Gottlieb Georgi, *Geographisch-physikalische und naturhistorische Beschreibung des Rußischen Reichs zur Übersicht bisheriger Kenntnisse von demselben*, III/4 (Königsberg, 1800), p. 953.
34 R. Hoeppli and I. Chiang, 'The Louse, Crab-louse and Bedbug in Old Chinese Medical Literature with Special Consideration on Phtiriasis', *Chinese Medical Journal*, LVIII (1940), pp. 338–62.
35 Hoffmann, 'Ernstes und Kurioses', pp. 95–136; Boynton, 'The Bed-bug', pp. 13–31; J.F.D. Shrewsbury, *The Plague of the Philistines and Other Medical-historical Essays* (London, 1964).
36 Margit Szöllösi-Janze, 'Pesticides and War: The Case of Fritz Haber', *European Review*, IX (2001), p. 100.
37 Hoffmann, 'Ernstes und Kurioses', pp. 95–136.
38 Szöllösi-Janze, 'Pesticides and War', p. 100.
39 Ibid., p. 107.
40 Ferdinand Flury and Albrecht Hase, 'Blausäurederivate zur Schädlingsbekämpfung', *Münchener Medizinische Wochenschrift*, LXVII (1920), pp. 779–80.
41 Szöllösi-Janze, 'Pesticides and War', p. 107.
42 Robert L. Metcalf, 'A Century of DDT', *Journal of Agricultural and Food Chemistry*, XXI (1973), p. 511.
43 Clive Boase, 'Bed Bugs (Hemiptera: Cimicidae): An Evidence-based Analysis of the Current Situation', in *Proceedings of the Sixth*

International Conference on Urban Pests, ed. William H. Robinson
and Dániel Bajomi (Veszprém, 2008).

44 Theodor Kröger, *Das vergessene Dorf* (Berlin, 1934), p. 114.

45 Heinrich Kemper, 'Die Bettwanze und ihre Bekämpfung',
Hygienische Zoologie, IV (1936), p. 89.

46 Anonymous, 'Company Introduces First Bed Bug Detecting Dog',
Hotel and Motel Management, 31 January 2006.

8 THE OTHER BUG

1 Elihu D. Richter and Yael Stein, 'Incitement, Hate Language,
and Terror: An Epidemiologic Perspective', in *The Changing
Forms of Incitement to Terror and Violence: The Need for a New
International Response*, ed. Alan Baker (Jerusalem, 2012),
pp. 127–40; available at http://jcpa.org, accessed
17 September 2017.

2 Sarah Jansen, *'Schädlinge': Geschichte eines wissenschaftlichen und
politischen Konstrukts, 1840–1920* (Frankfurt, 2003).

3 Nico Voigtländer and Hans-Joachim Voth, 'Nazi Indoctrination
and Anti-Semitic Beliefs in Germany', *Proceedings of the National
Academy of Sciences*, CXII (2015), pp. 7931 6.

4 Paul Lawrence Rose, *Richard Wagner und der Antisemitismus* Zürich,
1999).

5 'Antisemitismus bis 1945', http://de.wikipedia.org, accessed
10 November 2017.

6 Norman M. Naimark, *Fires of Hatred: Ethnic Cleansing in
Twentieth-century Europe* (Cambridge, MA, 2002).

7 Joanna Tokarska-Bakir, 'The Figure of the Bloodsucker in Polish
Religious, National and Left-wing Discourse, 1945–1946: A Study
in Historical Anthropology', *Dapim: Studies on the Holocaust*, XXVII
(2013), pp. 75–106.

8 Nyota Thun, *Ich – so groß und überflüssig: Wladimir Majakowski –
Leben und Werk* (Düsseldorf, 2000).

9 Lawrence Wright, *Warm and Snug: The History of the Bed* (London,
1962), p. 158.

10 Johann Heinrich Jördens, *Entomologie und Helminthologie des menschlichen Körpers, oder Beschreibung und Abbildung der Bewohner und Feinde desselben unter den Insekten und Würmern* (Hof, 1801), p. 36.

11 J.F.D. Shrewsbury, *The Plague of the Philistines and Other Medical-historical Essays* (London, 1964), p. 152.

12 Ruth Park, *The Harp in the South* (Sydney, 1948), p. 116.

13 Albrecht Hase, *Die Bettwanze (Cimex lectularius L.), ihr Leben und ihre Bekämpfung* (Berlin, 1917), p. 128.

9 BUGGING FORECAST: UNKNOWN, DISLIKED, OCCASIONALLY INTIMATE?

1 Ruth Park, *The Harp in the South* (Sydney, 1948), p. 115.

2 Sheldon Lou, *Sparrows, Bedbugs, and Body Shadows: A Memoir* (Honolulu, HI, 2005), pp. 90–94.

3 Ibid., p. 96.

4 J. A. Howe, *The Bug Man* (Kindle, 2015).

5 Friedrich S. Bodenheimer, *Materialien zur Geschichte der Entomologie bis Linné*, vol. I (Berlin, 1928).

6 John Keogh, *Zoologica Medicinalis Hibernica* (Dublin, 1739).

7 May Berenbaum, *Bugs in the System: Insects and their Impact on Human Affairs* (New York, 1995), p. 172.

8 Hans-Joachim Hoffmann, 'Ernstes und Kurioses über Wanzen – ein Heteropterologisches Panoptikum', *Denisia*, XIX (2006), p. 104.

9 Alexander Moszkowski, *Flächenwesen und Schattenwanderungen* (Berlin, 1922).

10 Henry Mayhew, *London Labour and the London Poor*, vol. III (London, 1861–2), p. 17.

11 Ibid.

12 John Southall, *A Treatise of Buggs* (London, 1730), p. 43.

Select Bibliography

Bello, Paul J., *The Bed Bug Combat Manual* (Bloomington,
    IN, 2011)
Boase, Clive, and Richard Naylor, 'Bed Bug Management',
    in *Urban Insect Pests: Sustainable Management Strategies*,
    ed. Partho Dhang (Wallingford, 2014), pp. 8–22
Borrel, Brooke, *Infested: How the Bed Bug Infiltrated Our Bedrooms
    and Took Over the World* (Chicago, IL, 2015)
Boynton, L.O.J., 'The Bed-bug and the "Age of Elegance"', *Furniture
    History*, I (1963), pp. 15–31
Busvine, James R., *Insects and Hygiene* (London, 1966)
Carayon, Jacques, 'Insémination extragénitale traumatique',
    in *Traité de zoologie, anatomie, systématique, biologie*, ed. Pierre-Paul
    Grassé, VIII/5-A (Paris, 1977), pp. 349–90
Cassis, G., and G. F. Gross, *Hemiptera: Heteroptera (Coleorrhyncha to
    Cimicomorpha)*, 27.3A of *Zoological Catalogue of Australia*,
    ed. W.W.K. Houston and G. V. Maynard (Melbourne, 1995)
Frisch, Karl von, *Zwölf kleine Hausgenossen* (Munich, 1940, revd 1976);
    trans. A. T. Sugar as *Twelve Little Housemates* (Oxford, 1978,
    repr. 2013)
Hase, Albrecht, *Die Bettwanze (Cimex lectularius L.): ihr Leben und
    ihre Bekämpfung* (Berlin, 1917)
Hoffmann, Hans-Joachim, 'Ernstes und Kurioses über Wanzen –
    ein Heteropterologisches Panoptikum', in *Hug the Bug: For Love of
    True Bugs: Festschrift zum 70. Geburtstag von Ernst Heiss*,
    ed. W. Rabitsch (Linz, 2006), pp. 95–136

Kemper, Heinrich, *Die Bettwanze und ihre Bekämpfung* (Leipzig, 1936)

—, *Die Tierischen Schädlinge im Sprachgebrauch* (Berlin, 1959)

Marlatt, Charles L., 'The Bedbug', [USDA] *Farmers' Bulletin*, 754 (14 October 1916)

Mayakovsky, Vladimir, *Klop* (Moscow, 1929)

Miller, N.C.E., *The Biology of the Heteroptera* (London, 1956)

Patton, Walter Scott, and Francis William Cragg, *A Textbook of Medical Entomology* (London, 1913)

Potter, Michael F., *The History of Bedbug Management: With Lessons from the Past* (Annapolis, MD, 2011)

Reinhardt, Klaus, ed., *Literarische Wanzen: Eine Anthologie. Nebst einer kleinen Natur- und Kulturgeschichte* (Berlin, 2014)

—, and Michael T. Siva-Jothy, 'Biology of the Bedbugs (Cimicidae)', *Annual Review of Entomology*, 52 (2007), pp. 351–74

Ryckman, Raymond E., and D. G. Bentley, 'Host Reactions to Bug Bites (Hemiptera, Homoptera): A Literature Review and Annotated Bibliography', *California Vector Views*, 26 (1979), pp. 1–49

Schaefer, Carl W., and Antonio Ricardo Panizzi, eds, *Heteroptera of Economic Importance* (Boca Raton, FL, 2000)

Schuh, Randall T., and James A. Slater, *True Bugs of the World (Hemiptera: Heteroptera): Classification and Natural History* (Ithaca, NY, 1995)

Service, Mike, *Medical Entomology for Students* (Cambridge, 2012)

Sinclair, Clive, *Bedbugs* (London, 1982)

Southall, John, *A Treatise of Buggs* (London, 1730)

Southwood, Richard T., and Dennis Leston, *Land and Water Bugs of the British Isles* (London, 1959)

Usinger, Robert Leslie, *Autobiography of an Entomologist* (San Francisco, CA, 1972)

—, *Monograph of Cimicidae (Hemiptera – Heteroptera)* (Lanham, MD, 1966, repr. 2007)

Weber, Hermann, *Biologie der Hemipteren* (Berlin, 1930)

READING FOR CHILDREN

Bueche, Shelley, *Bedbugs*, Parasites (New Haven, CT, 2005)
Gleason, Carrie, *Feasting Bedbugs, Mites and Ticks* (New York, 2010)
Jeffries, Joyce, *Bedbugs: Freaky Freeloaders that Feed on People* (New York, 2015)
Rhodes, Melody, and Edward Aish, *The Bedbug Who Wouldn't Bite* (Inglewood, NZ, 2009)

Associations and Websites

BEDBUGGER.COM
www.bedbugger.com
An entertaining website with a broad range of topics on bedbugs, from bites and hints on how to get rid of them to research and a guests' forum on infested hotels, photographs, videos and advertisements.

BED BUG WEB SITE
www.medent.usyd.edu.au/bedbug
A site run by the Department of Medical Entomology at Westmead Hospital of the University of Sydney and the Institute of Clinical Pathology and Medical Research, notable because all the facts on it are correct.

BRITISH BUGS
www.britishbugs.org.uk
Website with current information on British species of Heteroptera, including new records and an online identification guide. Also contains the newsletter *HetNews* and its predecessor *Heteropterists' Newsletter*.

EKKEHARD WACHMANN-ENTOMOLOGIE
http://ekkehard-wachmann.de/wanzen
A rich source of photographs of central European species of Heteroptera.

EUROPEAN BUGS
www.heteroptera.eu
Another good source of photographs of European species of
Heteroptera.

HETEROPTERON
www.heteropteron.de
Newsletter of the Arbeitsgruppe Mitteleuropäischer Heteropterologen
(Central European Society of Heteropterologists). In German.

THE BEDBUG FOUNDATION
http://bedbugfoundation.org/en/home
Website of a non-profit organization that informs about bedbug
biology and advises on the code of practice for bedbug control.

THE INTERNATIONAL HETEROPTERISTS' SOCIETY
www.ihs.myspecies.info
A society that promotes studies on taxonomy, distribution and
biology of Heteroptera.

TREE OF LIFE
www.tolweb.org/Hemiptera
Website listing all known evolutionary relationships among the true
bugs (Heteroptera).

Acknowledgements

I thank Mike Siva-Jothy, who hired me in 2002 to work on bedbugs. I got bitten and have never got rid of bedbugs since. He, and the members of his, and later our joint, lab were instrumental in propelling research on bedbugs – and with it propelled my interest into the bedbug's history and cultural relations. Most and foremost I wish to mention my friend Richard Naylor from CimexStore (UK), who also provided so many of the most beautiful photographs of this book, as well as Oliver Otti. Thank you, Rich, Mike and Otti. Then students who worked in our lab on various research projects were instrumental in generating some of the knowledge that I could write about here, particularly Adam Dobson, Toby Fountain, Aimee McTighe and Steph Myszka.

The Librarian of the Royal Entomological Society, Valerie McAtear, provided great help and made accessible the ancient books of the Society. Thank you, Val. I thank a countless number of people who took sufficient interest in the accumulating heap of bedbug anecdotes to continuously supply me with more episodes, pictures and website links. Such ineradicable help over many years was provided by Günter Köhler, Steffen Roth and Gregor Schulte. Many people, too many to be named here, willingly provided information of what must have appeared as strange requests concerning bedbugs in seemingly unrelated circumstances or helped to track down hidden copyright holders of various images.

Some of the ideas developed in this book have been initiated by the public readings of PariaCreation that I carried out with my friend Thomas Woitalla. Thank you, Thomas. I thank Jonathan R. Burt and Antje Graf for reading drafts of the entire manuscript and very helpful suggestions, Harry Gilonis for image searching and processing, Vi Nguyen, Adam Dobson and Biz Turnell for language editing and Amy Salter from Reaktion Books for several rounds of unbelievably careful proofreading. My final, big thank you goes to my daughter. She agreed to postpone our joint hiking holiday so that I could finalize the manuscript in due time. Thank you, Lina, my sweetheart.

Photo Acknowledgements

The author and publishers wish to express their thanks to the below sources of illustrative material and / or permission to reproduce it. Some locations are also given in the captions for the sake of brevity.

From *Die Arbeiter-Illustrierte Zeitung*, XII/35 (7 September 1933) – photo © The Heartfield Community of Heirs/VG Bild-Kunst, Bonn, 2017: p. 128; Archiv der Max-Planck-Gesellschaft, Berlin-Dahlem, reproduced by permission: p. 120; photos by or courtesy the author: pp. 9, 12, 21, 38, 39, 42, 50, 51, 52, 56, 79, 81, 83, 90, 98, 110 (right), 116, 121, 147, 148, 149, 153, 154, 157; from Friedrich Justin Bertuch, *Bilderbuch für Kinder: enthaltend eine angenehme Sammlung von Thieren, Pflanzen, Früchten, Mineralien . . .*, vol. III (Weimar, 1798): p. 54; from Émile Blanchard, *Histoire naturelle des insectes orthoptères, névroptères, hémiptères, hymén-optères, lépidoptères et diptères*, vol. III (Paris, 1851): p. 13; photo Mark Chappell, reproduced by kind permission: p. 26; courtesy Stevyn Colgan, reproduced by kind permission: p. 60; from John Curtis, *British Ento-mology, being illustrations and descriptions of the genera of insects found in Great Britain and Ireland . . .*, vol. VII (London, 1824): p. 16; from Michael S. Engel, 'A Stem-group Cimicid in Mid-Cretaceous Amber from Myanmar (Hemiptera: Cimicoidea)', *Alavesia*, no. 2 (2008): p. 25, top (image used by permission of Michael S. Engel, University of Kansas); photo © Ento-mart: p. 17; from C. L. Fletcher et al, 'Widespread Bullous Eruption Due to Multiple Bed Bug Bites', *Clinical and Experimental Dermatology*, XXVII/1 (January, 2002),© Elsevier: p. 99; from David A. Grimaldi, M. S. Engel et al., 'Fossiliferous Cretaceous amber from Burma (Myanmar): its rediscovery, biotic diversity, and paleontological significance', *American Museum Novitates*, no. 3361 (2002): p. 25, foot (image used by permission of Michael S. Engel, University of Kansas); illustration by Danny Hellman, reproduced by kind permission: p. 78; from *Hortus sanitatis: quatuor libris haec quae subsequuntur complectens* (Strasburg, 1536): p. 29; from Cecil G. Johnson, 'Thermograph Records in Rooms of some London Dwelling-houses throughout the Year 1935–36 and their Comparison with Temperatures Recorded on Out-door Meteorological Stations', *Journal of Hygiene*, vol. XXXVIII (1938): p. 110 (left); photo Katrine Kongshavn: p. 19; Library of Congress, Washington, DC (Prints and Photographs Division): pp. 36, 77 (William P. Gottlieb Collection); from [A.W. McKenny-Hughes], 'The Bed-bug, its Habits and Life History, and How to Deal with it', *Economic Series*, no. 5 (London: The British Museum [Natural History], 1913) – photo © The Trustees of the Natural History Museum, London: p. 6; from Ekkehart Malotki, *The Bedbugs' Night Dance and Other Hopi Tales of Sexual Encounter* (Lincoln, NE, published for Northern Arizona University by the University of Nebraska Press, 1995), reproduced by permission of the University of Nebraska Press: p. 76; from [Pietro Andrea Mattioli], *I Discorsi di M. Pietro Andrea Mattioli Sanese* [. . .] *ne I Sei Libri Di Pedacio Dioscoride Anazarbeo della materia Medicinale* (Venice, 1568): p. 97; courtesy Jan Michels, reproduced by kind permission: p. 68; from *Münchener Neueste Nachrichten* (25 December 1930), © Eberhard Spangenberg, reproduced by kind permission: p. 101; from 'Nadar' [Gaspard Félix Tournachon] and Charles Bataille, *La Grande symphonie héroïque des punaises* (Paris, 1877): p. 48; National Portrait Gallery, London: p. 32; photos Richard Naylor (CimexStore UK): pp. 20, 22, 23, 44, 45, 53, 57, 58, 82, 91, 92, 93, 94, 95 (foot), 96, 105; used with the permission of the Pacific Coast Entomological Society: p. 95 (top); photo Eva Panagiotakopulu (School of GeoSciences, University of Edinburgh) reproduced by kind permission: p. 28; from [G.W.F. Panzer], *Drury's Abbildungen und Beschreibungen exotischer Insekten mit fein illuminirten Kupfertafeln. Aus dem Englischen übersezt . . . von Georg Wolfgang Franz Panzer* (Nuremberg, 1785): p. 15; photos Milan Paunović: p. 104; from Heinz Schreckenberg, *The Jews in Christian Art: An Illustrated History* (New York, 1996), reproduced by permission of Bloomsbury Publishing

Index